SUMMA PUBLICATIONS, INC.

Thomas M. Hine
Publisher

William C. Carter
Editor-in-chief

Orders:
Box 20725
Birmingham, AL 35216

Editorial Address:
3601 Westbury Road
Birmingham, AL 35223

FRONTIERS

FRONTIERS

by

Michel Butor

Translated and with an introduction by
Elinor S. Miller
Embry-Riddle Aeronautical University

Part III translated in collaboration with
Warren C. Miller

SUMMA PUBLICATIONS, INC.
Birmingham, Alabama
1989

Cover and frontispiece photographs by Annie Fiori

Cover design by Susan Dendy

CONTENTS

INTRODUCTION

MICHEL BUTOR, SINCE THE FIFTIES, HAS BEEN RECOGNIZED AS ONE OF the most important writers in the world, and yet he remains scarcely known to the English-speaking reader. Translations of his earlier works have gone out of print, and his more recent ones remain in limited editions. Professors of comparative literature, of contemporary world literature, of art, music, and their criticism, anxious to use his works with classes for non-francophone students, must resign themselves to other writers' more readily available translated works; the loss is the American students' and it is enormous.[1] Butor, first as writer of one of the most widely read "New Novels," then as collaborator with musicians and visual artists and creator of "stereophonic" writings, has never ceased experimenting with new and different forms. He has been called Janus, Red Indian, perpetual motion, titles to which has been recently added Proteus.[2] Deeply internalized, the classics of the world infuse his work through the fascinating and always valuable effects of deliberate interweaving of texts, even as he brings new understanding to the most experimental of recent works of art, music, literature, theatre, and philosophy.

Beyond the form and the explanatory value of his criticism of the works of others, the content itself is rich and varied. Through all his writing runs a subtext of reverence for life, not only human, through time and space, in all our foolish ways, but for animals, with us and extinct, and for the living natural world of plants and trees. Readily seen as an Athena of wisdom, Butor does not have a Western figure comprehensive enough to use as a label for this caring: we would need Christ and St. Francis and Jane Goodall and all the conservationists together. Albert Schweitzer perhaps comes the closest. Buddha will not quite do, as Butor's work clearly shows that, while recognizing that all does become dust again, he would prefer not to accept man's deliberate destruction of himself and of the living world. His work stands as his caring effort to prevent that destruction.

Butor the artist provides a virtually endless field of study; Butor the man is a complex combination of writer, academic, traveler, and dreamer. The idea that the biography of a writer is essential to literary criticism has been much battered about in the last century and up to current deconstructive positions. The New Critics, now probably the Old New Critics, disdained the writer's life, feeling the work should stand alone. Today we live with that self-contradictory term, post-modernism, and some New Old New Critics insist that biography should be scrupulously avoided, while a glossary full of other critics would bring certain aspects of the biography back into discussion, sometimes to prove that the writer did not recognize what he was actually saying, or what his text ultimately meant. All these positions shed more or less light on the text in question, depending on whether the critic is more or less interested in the text itself as opposed to his own critical theory. Butor's writings can stand perfectly well alone, and he provides in them as much autobiographical information as may be pertinent to the particular work. However, to clarify and simplify the necessarily brief introduction to his work here, it seems useful to provide some hooks to hang the works on.[3]

Butor was not born in Paris, but moved there as a child. When the war was finally over, he completed his thesis on "Mathematics and the Idea of Necessity," under Gaston Bachelard, but failed the comprehensive state examination, the agrégation. No one familiar with the ultra-conservative nature of academe would be surprised that Butor's philosophy did not follow acceptable canonized lines.[4] Fortunately for the reading public, anger and disappointment over being refused prompted him to take teaching assignments, first outside Paris at Sens, and then in Egypt, at the town of El Minya south of Cairo, and next at the University of Manchester in England. Returning to Paris, Butor frequented the writers who came to be known as the New Novelists: Nathalie Sarraute, Alain Robbe-Grillet, Claude Simon, and others. He continued to travel whenever possible, always back to Italy, but also during teaching assignments in Salonika, Greece, and in Geneva.

The surprising success of his third novel, *Change of Heart* (1957), which depends on his knowledge of Rome, marks a distinct turning point in his life. The first, *Milan Passage* (1954), had been favorably received by the critics, but like most of the "New Novels," did not sell well. *Time Schedule* (1956) attracted even more attention and later was awarded a prize, but it was *Change of Heart* which won the important Prix Renaudot and brought Butor to international attention and his share of the alternating acclaim and rage directed at the New Novelists. Since that time he and they have spent many interviews, seminars, and colloquia rejecting any concept of themselves as a group or movement. Indeed, the only position they admit to having in common is that they can no longer write novels in the traditional form, with defined characters, chronologically presented action, and specific point of view. The forms they developed for their writing since have that negative in common, but little else. Butor's first collection of essays, *Repertory,* won the prize for literary criticism the same year his fourth novel, *Degrees,* was published (1959), this time with Gallimard, one of the major publishers, where Butor remains on contract for his major works; this represents success for a French writer.

Married to Marie-Jo, whose name, along with those of their four daughters, is a constant in succeeding semi-autobiographical works, Butor continued his incredibly prolific publication while traveling ever farther and longer. His first trip to the United States was as visiting professor, a semester at Bryn Mawr and a summer at Middlebury, and he has since been visiting professor at the Universities of Buffalo, New Mexico, Oklahoma, Louisville, and others, and has presented seminars and colloquia all over the country. Between these terms he lived in Berlin on a Ford Foundation grant, traveled in Bulgaria, Yugoslavia, the near East, Russia, Japan, southeast Asia, Brazil, New Zealand, Mexico, Guatamala, and Australia, where he spent a year as visiting professor. Meanwhile he revealed the overall format of his major works: five of each kind was enough. We now have five *Repertories* of essays, five "stereophonic" works, more or less destined for live performance, five *Stuff of Dreams* of dream sequences, four *Illustrations* on visual artists, three *Spirit of the Place,* and the fourth is described in the Postscript to *Frontiers,* two *Envoys* of poems, two *Improvisations* drawn from his lectures on individual authors, with more planned, as detailed in the Postscript. The bibliography reveals that in addition to these series, he writes about art, music, and literature in conventional prose, while creating works of art with visual artists which are exhibited at the Pompidou Museum, not the least remarkable being the *Bicentennial Kit* with Jacques Monory. Amid the travel and the publications, another turning

point can be identified as his move to Nice in 1970, away from Paris, a
move which he discusses in *Frontiers*.

Firmly established and internationally renowned, Butor was nonetheless denied the title of Professor on his defense of the doctoral disserta-
tion in 1973, indicating a sad lack of perception on the part of the university
committee.[5] He taught for a while at the University of Nice but then, as
Professor at the University of Geneva, he was for years content to commute
between Nice and Geneva, thus continually crossing the Swiss frontier.
His beautiful home, "The Antipodes," lies between the silence of the site of
a 400,000-year-old community, the Terra Amata, and the noise of today's
city and port, humming with modernity. This year he has moved tempo-
rarily closer to Geneva, still in France, but on the frontier. Fortunately for
us in the United States, he continues to respond to the demand here for
visiting professorships, and it is a rare year that his voice is not heard
somewhere in the United States.

The best biography is provided by his works. *Milan Passage*
presents the isolation of life in a Paris apartment; *Time Schedule* plunges us
into the British fog, cold, darkness, and industrial wasteland. *Portrait of
the Artist as a Young Monkey* tells us of his experiences in Germany. The
first two in the *Spirit of the Place* series take us with him to Egypt, Greece,
Italy, then the Far East and Far West, and in the third, *Boomerang,* we learn
of his observations on Brazil and Singapore as well as Australia. *Mobile*
gives us his vision of the whole United States. Each new work gives us
further insight into his life, usually as spent in another different country.

His works of literary or artistic criticism do not offer so much biographical information, but we learn from them respect for Butor the reader,
observer, listener, the critic who invariably leaves us with the desire to go
forth and read the books, see the paintings, listen to the music. He states
this precept in *Frontiers:* "The reader of the article, of the study will probably want to go plunge into this work [the subject of the critic's writing]—
and that, of course, is the purpose the critic's work ought to serve" (p. 51).

It is impossible to examine here all or even a representative number
of these works. Indeed, again and again critics approaching his extensive
publication limit themselves to one aspect, one genre (if one can apply that
term meaningfully to Butor's writings), one theme. So too here we will try
to present only an idea of one example of each of the major trends. The
choice is very difficult for the Butor scholar dedicated to the belief that every

one of his works deserves ever more critical attention, but some do demand it more loudly than others, because of their reception by the public, positive and negative.

Change of Heart both infuriated and captivated the public. It remains the prototype of a novel written in the second person. Throughout, it is *you* who are in the train compartment, *you* who review *your* wife's failings versus *your* mistress's fascinatingly exotic association with Rome, and *you* who return from Rome to Paris without breaking up *your* marriage. The presentation is completely achronological, as are one's or your memories. The reader finds himself experiencing the trip, remembering all the other trips, puzzling perhaps to recall exactly what happened when and where, and eventually recognizing that he, with the protagonist, has gone through a change of heart. Recently a feminist position has been stated about *Change of Heart,* resentment against the male "you" shell into which the female reader is forced, uncomfortable especially as the protagonist's representation to himself (to "us") of both women in his life is painfully stereotyped.[6] It is true that the "you" constrains the reader to think with the narrator even more intimately than is ordinarily the case. Certainly the protagonist suffers from machismo, but Butor as certainly does not. Indeed it would seem possible that the very constraint imposed on the reader by the "you" might have brought some male reader somewhere to the realization that his own understanding of women in real life resembled this sad protagonist's.

Butor's experimentation with "stereophonic" works began with *Mobile,* his "Study for a representation of the United States," typographically varied, in margins and print. The second, *6,810,000 Liters of Water a Second,* is subtitled "Stereophonic Study." This work, on Niagara Falls, includes careful instructions for the reader for adjusting the sound, as if actually on a stereo, and it has been broadcast on radio. In the book, sound effects are written in, and there are parenthetical sections which the "hurried reader" may omit, Butor says, while listening to the thoughts and speeches of the series of characters. The overall structure is provided by the year: month by month the flowers and weather change, and within that, the time of day, from dawn through the middle of the night. The alphabet provides continuity among the characters: the newlyweds are Abel and Betty one month, Arthur and Bertha the next; C and D are an older married couple returning for a second honeymoon; there are a black couple, unhappy lovers, and men and women alone. Throughout, a Reader recites Chateaubriand's 1797 description of Niagara, first in its entirety, then gradually recombining its words in constant permutation, until the end, where he reads the 1801 version of the text. The "stereophonic" effects are readily imagined, and the reader who has never seen Niagara comes to know it intimately, as he never could on a single honeymoon visit. More, he sees it through Butor's eyes, as the honeymooners leave with the same hopes the older married couples no longer have, as the blacks and whites are still separated, the lonesome still alone. This critic sees it as a prime example of Butor's deep appreciation for natural wonders, along with his empathy for all humanity.

The series of *Repertories* contains essays in relatively conventional prose on a wide variety of subjects, from Balzac and Proust to Mondrian and Rothko. In some cases the essays are revisions, as described in *Frontiers,* of preliminary drafts published with small presses, as, for example, the piece, *Vanity.* Published in 1980 by Balland, subtitled "A Conversation in the Maritime Alps," *Vanity* reappears, slightly revised, in *Repertory V.* The changes are mainly in the conclusion, where Butor has deleted the personal experience of a close brush with death recounted by one of the speakers. In its place he has developed further an intercalated quotation from Chateaubriand's *Life of Rancé,* on the skull of his former mistress, which Rancé supposedly kept in his monastic cell for meditation. The new version thus becomes more universal, first through Chateaubriand of the nineteenth century, then through Rancé of the seventeenth, and by implication on back through all the monks, whose world view is essential to the whole subject of the vanities. Also added in the later version are stage directions, sound effects, a passing butterfly, which enliven the scene and increase the reverberations among the different parts of the text. The ultimate point of this conversation on the vanities, clarified and emphasized in the revised version, is the function of the artist in society: to transform, to cure. The speakers recognize that if they were to succeed in their attempts, they would be suppressing their own individuality as artists, as the ones who are, exactly, different from everyone else. However, they recognize also that their efforts are always in vain. Here as elsewhere, while specifically rejecting the concept of the artist as *engagé* in the political arena, Butor is still always concerned with human society, its sins of commission and omission.

It should be noted that as each series of five progresses, the works refer more often to previous works of Butor. Techniques of what he calls collage, folding a text of another into his own, increase in complexity as he adds his own earlier texts also. The first *Stuff of Dreams* is composed of five dream sequences, each an intricate combination of texts he has read, texts he has written, all set within the dream. Even the most accomplished reader of Butor is thrown into a frenzy of research, endeavoring to seize and place all the references. In the fourth, *Quadrupled Base,* there is a thread of a plot—dreamlike—in which a composer is commissioned to write an opera, restricted only to one that is *not* a Faust. It is useful to know that one of Butor's collaborative works outside the series of five was *Your Faust* with Henri Pousseur. This work theoretically has at least twenty-five different endings, as the audience must decide at various points what the next action is to be: will Faust save Marguerite or not?[7] References to this work are incorporated into *Quadrupled Base* in the collage manner, along with eleven other themes. Indeed, the structure of this work is that of serial music, with the carefully designed arrangement juxtaposing the description of a woods animal to a fragment of conversation between the composer and producer. Butor has used other musical forms in the past: canon as early as *Time Schedule,* ground bass in *6,810,000 Liters of Water a Second,* and theme and variations in the *Dialogue with 33 Variations by Beethoven on a Diabelli Waltz,* among others. Once perceived, the serial music structure of *Quadrupled Base* enables the reader to enjoy the effects of the juxtapositions all the more.

Among Butor's collaborative writings about and with visual artists, normally published by small presses or in de luxe editions, one of the most extraordinary is the *Bicentennial Kit.* Issued in 1975 for the United States bicentennial, it is hardly a book, but rather a box. Butor had it designed for the purpose in exactly the appropriate American blue plastic, with layers and compartments to fit the objects he has assembled. The collection includes a sheriff's badge, a mashed Coke top, a Shaker peg, different colored masks for a bicentennial party, and plasticized popcorn. There is one of these souvenir toys in which snow floats around in a viscuous liquid, in this case of course, over the Statue of Liberty. There are documents: various proposals for a better division of the fifty states, a flyer from the Washington wax museum, a WANTED poster for Patty Hearst, memorabilia from the 1876 centennial celebration. There are twenty serigraphs by Jacques

Monory and a Catalogue text describing all the objects. There Butor describes, satirizes, or extolls the United States. Interspersed are Benjamin Franklin-like sayings for cross-stitch samplers, and poems on a "blue" expression, such as "blue stocking," "to look blue," "once in a blue moon." Number 3 is an off-print of Butor's own article on Marcel Duchamp, which supports his use of "itself" and "ready-made" in the Catalogue. Number 11 is a restaurant paper place mat with pictures of all the Presidents; the text in the Catalogue details spots on each: coffee for George Washington, ink for Jefferson, watercress and blood for Lincoln, until finally onion soup and blood for Kennedy, syrup for Johnson and axle grease for Nixon. As in *Mobile,* Butor demonstrates a much deeper knowledge of our country and of its history than most of us have. His caring for the oppressed appears in his inclusion of Indian legends, beliefs that some day the white man will just go away. And he forces us to recognize the failings of our revered founding fathers by citing Thomas Jefferson's letter requesting from France some talented slaves in order to have "a little music in the evenings." There is truth, good and bad, about the United States in this blue plastic box.

The third in the *Spirit of the Place* series, *Boomerang,* utilizes texts from the *Bicentennial Kit* in its blue sections—blue because *Boomerang* adds a new element to Butor's experiments in form. The first *Spirit of the Place* (1958) already used open paragraphs with intercalated texts. The second, entitled in French *Où,* which can only be translated *Where/Or* because the accent on *where* is cancelled to create *or,* added italicized titles among the varying margins and typefaces, among fragmented sentences or whole conversations mingled with single words and poetry. *Boomerang* is composed of one or two blocks of red, blue, or black text arranged on the two open pages. Running titles of related words (flora and fauna, place names, constellations) alternating with identifying symbols are printed across the top, center, or bottom of the page. The name of the author of an intercalated text appears in boldface somewhere within or near the citation. The colored and varied typography not only exemplifies Butor's concept of the book itself as an art object, but aids the reader through the global labyrinth.

And it is global. Five regions are treated: (1) "Letters from the Antipodes," a play on words with the name of his home in Nice, is the longest, composed of his letters to his wife during the second trip to Australia, and of Australian documents. (2) Excerpts from the *Bicentennial*

Kit deal with the United States, with echoes of *Mobile*. (3) "Archipelago Shopping" reflects the bazaars of Hong King and Singapore, and (4) "Transatlantic Carnival" is a succession of carnival floats, from Nice to Rio de Janiero. (5) "The Party in My Absence" is from *Where/Or,* and refers to a potlatch Butor was invited to in British Columbia, which ultimately did not take place, while his family went to the Zuni festival he had seen during a previous stay in New Mexico. In addition, there are two subsidiary regions: (A) scenes from the "Gallant New Indies" of Rameau, and (B) "Jungle," made up of Buffon"s descriptions of animals, both of which Butor calls "well done," in the culinary sense, as indeed the very first page of the book reveals: the animal described metamorphosizes gradually from a kangaroo to an elephant, to some kind of carniverous marsh beast, and finally to a hibernating solitary bear.

These texts may be interrupted for several pages or be cut off in mid-thought, to pick up at a different point on the following page, much later, or never.[8] The selection of texts and their juxtaposition has kept many critics very busy creating charts and diagrams to explain the organization and enable the reader to profit as fully as possible from the work. It is, however, possible simply to read through it. Through the kaleidoscopic shifts in color, titles, regions, authors, and texts, Butor himself is revealed. We learn of course about Australia, myth and reality, about the American influence it has felt and survived, about customs of the Far East and the internationality of carnival, and about the writer's real-life experiences and feelings while so far from his family. There is the erudition we have come to expect, encyclopaedic knowledge, vivid description of people and places, wit and humor, as he juxtaposes personals from the newspaper, wondering if any two lonely hearts will manage to get together. It is especially through the juxtapositions that his deep and persistent concern appears, concern for the disparagement, degradation, and destruction of so-called primitive peoples. The life story of a wealthy philanthropist follows a newspaper account of aborigine children, sometimes three to a bed, dying of measles in an inadequately equipped hospital. A flyer detailing the luxurious delights of a resort, where tables are spread with delicacies day and night, precedes an aborigine legend of the struggle to maintain control of the tortoise supply, their only nourishment. Throughout there is the caring about all people, all animals, all life.

Butor has said, "To leave a trace of one's passage is to belong to the place, is to become Roman oneself, Athenian, or Cairote" (*Repertory IV,* 27). In this sense Butor has certainly become a citizen of most countries in the world, become American, Thai, Australian aborigine, as well as Nice-ite, for he has left traces. No reader of Butor can visit Niagara, Rome, San Marco, and Australia, without seeing through his eyes: his "trace" is engraved not on tombs as in Rome nor on birch bark as by the aborigine, but in the minds of his readers.[9]

To set about reading all Butor would be rather like attacking all Balzac, all Hugo, all Zola. In a world that no longer devotes time even to all Proust, it seems futile to recommend the effort. And yet, to share Butor's vision of the world through his art is to enrich one's life, to render living in that world more endurable.

∞ ∞ ∞

Butor speaks in *Frontiers* of translations he has made to fit different contexts and states "a translation can be faithful to different degrees" (52). He, as an artist, has the freedom to do exactly as he pleases. The common translator does not, and the operational principle applied to this work has been fidelity first to meaning. This translator would not have pretended to turn Butor's poetry into English without the collaboration of a poet; even so, decisions have been based almost exclusively on meaning rather than on poetic sensibility. Rhythm is usually lost, and rhyme, as for example in the second text when "enfance/souffrance" has to become "childhood/ suffering." Similarly, in the first text the very effective repetition in "Déraisonne, démonte, détourne, dédouble, déplore, détecte," cannot be rendered in English without altering the meaning. The wit in "mineur" and "démineur," depending on the wide difference in the two meanings of "mine," cannot be so succinctly put in English, and the "taupes philo-sophiques" would demand an explanatory note without the addition of "university," unnecessary in the original. Expressions in the pattern "between" two things, which have a specific meaning, as "between two wars" refers to the period 1918-39, and "between dog and wolf," which means twilight, have been dealt with as well as possible to retain meaning and poetry. Whoever reads a translation makes a leap of faith; let this hand-wringing by the translator-traitor suffice to justify it.

∞ ∞ ∞

This book, *Frontiers,* serves as an intriguing, tempting introduction to Butor's work. The form—conversations and examples—allows Butor to illustrate his particular approach to writing, to offer some quasi-autobiographical information, and to develop the particular theme of frontiers, seeing himself, the writer, as a "porous frontier," through which literature, art, culture, and sites pass and are transformed.

The form has appeared before, among the many interviews and conversations published over the last thirty years. It suits Butor's goal of "off-centering" (59, 61-63), of diverting action away from the established monopoly. In this case the great Parisian publishers are the focus, since he often utilizes small, provincial, sometimes foreign publishers. "What is important is that this fabric [of small publishers] exist, that the Great Parisian machines do not end up being the only ones" (62). *Frontiers* is not one of the major works Butor is committed to give to Gallimard, exactly one of "the great Parisian machines," but rather a freeze-frame stage, enabling the reader to take part in the development of the major works. It is the case that most of the texts have been previously published in one form or another, and Butor outlines in the "Postscript" his future publishing plans for some of these. However, as he notes there, his published texts function "like a sort of attic," where "texts go to sleep . . . but they dream" (121). Examination of earlier statements of his publishing plans reveals the works do not always issue forth in the planned marching order, and one should not expect them to, given the nature of dreams.

Further, this form allows focus on this particular stage of the texts included. Those Butor has chosen for *Frontiers* are excellent examples of his technique of revising, reworking, and especially resetting the texts from the attic in new rooms, in new designs and colors. Christian Jacomino, his interlocutor, remarks the difficulty a reader, even an academic, finds in keeping abreast of Butor's enormous productivity (60-61). The search for the provenance of the twelve "Examples" in *Frontiers* has led through catalogues of art exhibits, libretti for musical scores, a Japanese publication, and the results must still be essentially provisional. It has not always been possible to consult the apparently original version of a text, but a sample of a few of the wide span of sources for his collection should be of interest.[10]

For example: I, "Self-portrait of the 70's," appeared first as part of a much longer poem, "Project Blues" in *Approach Works*. The lines of our poem were there distributed among lines on a number of different themes: imaginary machines and imaginary works of art in literature, Butor's family dreaming of a new house, bits of personal letters apologizing for not having completed a piece of writing, and others. As so often in Butor, differing margins correspond to particular lines of thought: our poem is in lines beginning either at the first or second left-hand margin. Then, in Butor's book of conversations with Michel Launay, *Resistances,* published in 1983, both "Project Blues," in the short form of "Self-Portrait" in *Frontiers,* and II, "Before the Dialogue of the Living," each divided into sections, alternate as epigraphs throughout. Minor variants between these two texts among the versions demonstrate Butor's careful rearrangement of texts to meet his differing needs. The interconnections among his works multiply if one considers that the lines titled in *Frontiers* "Before the Dialogue of the Living" could be the same as a piece by that name written in collaboration with the artist Henri Maccheroni, and that the conversation called *Vanity* took place among the living artist Maccheroni, the living writer Michel Launay, and the living traveler Butor.

VII, "Between the Drops" appeared first in *Men at Work,* published in January 1985, the same year *Frontiers* appeared in the fall. Our version has seventeen variants, minor deletions or substitutions, indicative of a thoughtful revision. "Sounds of the Forest," mentioned in "Between the Drops," is the text Butor is writing on a tree in a photograph in the 1982 issue of *World Literature Today.* A brief version was published in *Express* in 1983, which does not use any of the lines quoted in *Frontiers.* A text by the same name figures in an art exhibit catalogue of Patrice Pouperon in 1984, interestingly enough published in Italian translation the same year. Then a long poem in seven sections of seven lines each, with the same name, appeared in *Men at Work,* and our lines are included there, unchanged.

Also mentioned in "Between the Drops" is "The Ballad of Iris' Scarf." This is a poem published in *Express* with the explanatory note:

> Vincent Bioulès was one of the first to glue strips of paper on canvas and unglue them after painting, thus obtaining unpainted or uncolored reserves, with very uneven edges. Working on repetitions at

the beginning or at the end of lines (a line of verse, according to
Mallarmé, being the "perfect line"), rhymes of all sorts, I wanted to
create for him a text in stripes, a spectrum with its bands, like those
which permit us to analyze the composition of stars. As the colors
mixed together more and more to create a white light in the night,
reproducing the famous experiment of Newton's disk, I was able to turn
this ballad into a small homage to this great and daring artist. (48)

This note on Bioulès's technique in painting and his own in writing adds to
the subject matter treatment in "Between the Drops" and gives some idea of
Butor's myriad approaches to art criticism.

VIII, "Saga" appeared first in limited edition with an engraving by
Gregory Masurovsky, as performed in 1976 under the name of "Zornagora
(A Saga)" written "with and for" Jacques Guiyonnet as a "sound fiction for
full orchestra and recitant." The text and some of the orchestral score were
published accompanying conversations in *Traveller at the Wheel* in 1979.
Our text is a profound revision of these earlier versions.

IX, "The 53 Stages of the Tokaïdo" is the twenty-first chapter of
"Floatings from East to West," to have been published in 1982 by Asahi
Publishers of Japan. Nine of the texts were published in English translation
in 1981-82, and Butor planned to offer a bilingual edition beginning with
the end of the last chapter of the Japanese text, since it would be read from
right to left, starting thus in the middle of the book. With the French text set
in normal order, beginning in the middle of the book, the "53 Stages"
would be both first and last.[11]

The wide variety of these works exemplifies the universal interests
of Butor, while illustrating his techniques of rearrangement and revision,
and further demonstrates the impossibility of neatly categorizing his works.
We might expect to find specifically autobiographical pieces here in
Frontiers, since Jacomino's stated purpose is to discuss the state of contemporary literature with Butor because he seems "more than anyone . . . aware
of his place in a world already saturated with writing" (42). There are
indeed indications by Butor of "his place," and in addition throughout the
conversations he refers to certain critical periods of his life. Yet the text,
"Self-Portrait" is "of the seventies" and not of himself. In any case he has
stated on a number of different occasions that in descriptions of himself written by others he scarcely recognizes himself, and certainly not

descriptions of his works. Here, among the vivid and surprising physical images of the poem, hardly flattering, are impressions of his approach to writing and his indomitable hope. He portrays himself as seeking "chinks in the Iron and Bamboo curtains" and "the reform of human understanding." VI, "In the Meantime," appears also somewhat autobiographical, a meditation on passing time. The individual changes, and while some enemies have worn themselves out, new ones have appeared. It is Butor's vision of the world and knowledge of history that provoke his remarking that the incessant war has changed the targets of the missiles and that the future has changed color as a maple does in autumn. One need not remember all the way back to World War I to recognize how many times those targets have changed and how differently the future has been imagined over such a short period of time. Thus the autobiographical elements in these two pieces are subordinate to a larger vision.

In VII, "Between the Drops," we see a particular aspect of his personal determination, giving the reader a very clear picture of his everyday life. The serious treatment of the artist Bioulès is intercalated, almost obscured, by the setting in which Butor finds himself as he tries to write. From one office to the other, in train or plane, in a cafe or restaurant, he manages to collect his impressions, thoughts, and finally the text to send Bioulès for the exposition. His functioning as an artist in the midst of this—in transit, as he says—remains one of his most remarkable achievements.

This whole work is quite naturally full of frontiers: in music, art, literature, language, and society, many of which are reflected in the four texts specifically about frontiers: "Rain on the Frontiers," "Bridges," "Post No Bills," and "Meditations on the Frontier."

In regard to music, Butor speaks in the conversations of contemporary music as the product of musicians' having recognized that silence is an integral part of their art, together with increased acceptance of new sounds. He sees this recognition and acceptance as the crossing of frontiers (40-41). In "Post No Bills" if we put our ear to the dividing wall we can hear bits of sounds from the other side, lute concerts in an antique mode: music crosses the frontier. At the very end of "Meditations," the frontier is seen as a vibratory membrane, at once producing and receiving the sound.

Art is treated in the conversations as Butor describes photography as the art of framing, a sort of decoupage, and explores the technique of collage as used by Braque and Picasso (49). Here the frontier crossed is between the work and the world, a theme treated in the "Free" and "Deep Frontiers" of "Meditations," where it gives rise to the splendid image of a frontier made of flowers.

Since one of Butor's techniques which has caused the most critical flurry is his use of citations, intercalation of texts, within his own and within each other, it is inevitable that much of the conversation should be dedicated to this process and its effects. Butor likes to think of his own texts' circulating among those of other writers, the end being "the realization of a myth," the myth of becoming someone else. As his texts blend with others, he feels he loses his identity, crosses the frontier which bounds one individual from another (51-52). The texts in *Frontiers*, interestingly enough, do not offer immediate examples of intertextuality, other than the myth of Icarus in "Bridges." "Post No Bills" is punctuated by warnings to someone adventuring to the other side: "Not a sound!" "Look out!" "Turn around!" inserted among the descriptions, but this is a second voice rather than an intercalated text.[12] The general idea of crossing the frontier to the Other is picked up in two of the texts: in "Post No Bills" the superstition is held by those on the other side that they cannot make love well without a glance from those on this side. Then the first three segments of "Meditation" dwell on the existence of the Other as essential to our own. These instances are closely related to one of Butor's most seriously continued themes, that we are all one.

Frontiers of language occur in the conversations relative to the question of the values of the speech of doctor and patient. Butor points out with pleasure that contemporary art has rejected the Freudian position, rigidly maintained by present-day psychiatry, that only the doctor's words have true value (48-49). There is a wonderful reflection of this determination (by psychiatrists) to keep the frontier fortified in "Post No Bills." Here the police of the other side have convinced themselves they are machines, using appropriate vocabulary to describe themselves and their bodily functions. They provide a perfect case for Freudian analysis, which, of course, would totally miss the point. There are moments when Butor's view of physicians is very like Molière's. Then in "Free Frontier" of "Meditation" he considers the shifts in meaning between "right" and "left" in their relation to "East" and "West," where the right or East has gradually, through centralization, eaten up the left or West, which was once not so much the other side of a frontier but the land without frontiers.

As for the frontiers of society, the conversations treat political involvement, or lack of it, by authors and intellectuals (59-60), the loss of the American West as a last frontier, together with the growth of big cities and the new opposition between city and country (42-43). This last is dwelt on particularly in the opposition between Paris and the rest of the country, as Butor develops his ideas on decentralization or, as he calls it here in a term borrowed from optics, off-centering. It becomes clear in "Meditations" that it is the center, the headquarters, whatever the political power is called, that is responsible for the continuation of walls, barriers, closed frontiers. In the "Thick" and "Crossed" segments Butor examines the attitude of the center, how, ever threatened by the unknown, its inhabitants feel the need for a closed frontier. The attitude on the frontier itself is totally opposite: the other side is as familiar as our own.

This particular theme is central to all four of these texts, that the center is the site of the fear, and consequently of the evil. In the texts it appears at the end of "Bridges," where we see the innocent Icarus destroyed by war profiteers in the form of hypocrites who gleefully rub their hands. In "Rain on the Frontiers" we do not know what desolate landscape we are in, only that it was not always thus, and that beyond it there is the other side. Here it is an unknown power that exerts the evil influence, not necessarily the center, but to go to the other side requires a dangerous deception of authorities of some kind. But the persona speaking is determined to go, will go, when the weather is good, because he is not afraid.

"Post No Bills" clearly presents an evil central authority, reminiscent of *1984*, become a surreal nightmare. In two long paragraphs we learn how it is behind the wall. All kinds of officials, from generals to gardeners, are busy about tasks not necessarily threatening in themselves until closely examined, and often grotesque and amusing. For example, we find the laureate authors writing best-sellers are presented exactly as are the bailiffs wiping off razor-sharp chains, and the accident-workers planning new ways to cause accidents rather than how to prevent them. We are not surprised to learn that our sense of foreboding was justified and that children expected to be good collaborators in "the great work of misery" are blinded early. The second paragraph gives us the distorted vision of the other side which we are permitted: people are smaller than we, animals larger than ours. The other side simply pretends the wall doesn't exist, whereas we are not allowed to look at or ask about it. The other side is the realm of those policemen-machines, but the police are also harsh on our side. In each case the beliefs are fostered by official policy and propaganda, that of a center. This text very clearly gives us Butor's feelings about totalitarianism, xenophobia, and man's inhumanity to man, not only as represented by the Berlin Wall, but wherever they occur.

The last text on frontiers, "Meditation," examines them from every conceivable point of view, including the geographical and historical. The last ones offer a chronological sequence, as the redoubled frontier around a no-man's-land is gradually crossed, opened, and becomes habitable. Each of these four frontier texts ends with a plea for an end to barriers: may the rain wash them away, may we built bridges rather than walls, let us give to those on the other side the attention they need. Finally, at the end, we watch the metamorphosis of two frontier territories: they become lovers and dance, casting their shadows on the walls of Earth's cave. It is not impossible that Butor alludes to Plato's cave, as the dancers go forth to conquer space.

All of these frontiers, in music, art, literature, language, and society, are presented by the writer who considers himself to be a frontier, a "porous frontier." In *Frontiers* we have examples of the passage of all kinds of traffic through this porous frontier: literature, the visual arts, sites. Each changes, more or less, in the passage: Icarus, foolish youth of myth, brought down by pride, becomes the world brought down by foolish fear. The speakers from all parts of the compass in the "Song of the Rose of Voices" may not voice actual citations, but what they might have said: Butor weaves them together until the whole world sings one song. Molière in the "Distant Comedy" is condensed and glorified into a meta-Molière. Butor's view of Bioulès's winter scene allows us, the readers who have not seen the painting, to feel the cold, as Butor does as he decides it is now too cold to study the night sky outside: the stars are like "an appeal or regret." The study of Hiroshige takes us, as we pass through the porous frontier of Butor, into the artist's mind: he knows, and thus we do, what Hiroshige thought and dreamed. Since Hiroshige could not travel to the rest of the world beyond Kyoto, the plates he made over and over represent the global voyage, which explains why Fuji changes from right to left of the traveler within the series. Butor knows the artist dreamed not only of Japan, but of the whole world, as paradise.

Sites of course change as they pass through Butor's porous frontier. The beech trees on one side of the frontier are different from the oaks of the other, but they develop beyond mere beech trees into anti-oak, and "our roofs proclaim the superiority of tile over thatch." The particular frontiers could be any Butor has known, but he specifically names in "Meditation" the Berlin wall and 32nd parallel. The Butorian fantasy world behind the wall of "Post No Bills" is one of the clearest examples of change in passage through the porous frontier: who among us imagined the drab ugliness of the Berlin Wall as walling off a society transported in Hovercraft drawn by giant swans? Then in "Meditations" we finally find a world without frontiers where, free of governmental and administrative restrictions, once out of the cave, the natural goodness of humankind soars beyond the shadows to Platonic truth.

We would like to suggest that where the changes are the greatest lie Butor's deepest concerns. As exemplified in *Frontiers,* these would be the abolition of national barriers, as in the "Song of the Rose of Voices" and in the frontier of flowers in the "Meditations," the recognition of the whole world as paradise as in the "53 Stages," the acceptance of human beings by one another as in "Post No Bills," and the dancing couple of the "Meditations." Plato would not have asked more of those come forth from the cave than that they should "conquer space in their embraces."

The reader of Butor encounters new ways of seeing, feeling, and understanding. An analogy he might like would be to the scientist who looks for the first time through a microscope or, better, a telescope. His apprehension of the world is forever changed.

Notes

[1]In 1982 Leon S. Roudiez addressed this problem at the University of Oklahoma's Puterbaugh Conference dedicated that year to Butor: ". . . I must point to a weakness of the past, in English-speaking countries at least. The weakness I have in mind is due to a dearth of translations. It is a deplorable situation" (*World Literature Today* 226).

[2]Anna Otten, "Butor the Protean," presented at the Rollins College Southeast Conference on Foreign Languages and Literatures, 1988.

[3]Madeleine Santschi's *Voyage avec Michel Butor,* conversations in the format of *Frontiers,* provides the most perceptive biography and most open autobiography we have yet seen. It is not yet translated into English.

[4]In *Degrees* Butor presents very clearly the limitations of the French secondary school program: everyone reads the same parts of the same works on the same day.

[5]In the preface to a splendid critical work on the French baroque, Jacques Maurens states that Butor's works "did not have the good fortune to please the majority of members of the twelfth section. To write with brilliance did not make up for the offense done to university traditions. One suspects it was an aggravating circumstance, because Butor was not even included in the 'long' list" (Baïche i-ii).

[6]Mary Beth Pringle, "Re-examination of the characterizations of Henriette and Cécile relative to the 'vous' of *La Modification,*" paper presented at the Rollins College Southeast Conference of Foreign Languages and Literatures, 1988.

[7]Mary Lydon cites a scathing review of *Your Faust* as performed in Milan in 1969, where actors were placed in the audience to intervene at appropriate moments. "And the fraud was all the more glaring in Milan since the performance was in French and the various actors planted in the audience interrupted in the only language they could speak—French" (*World Literature Today* 278).

[8]In an interview Butor said that the texts were intended to be cut as in Balzac's *Departmental Museum,* "the challenge being to break where there was no possible logical reason" (Butor to Dean McWilliams and Elinor S. Miller, Nice, 1977).

[9]We have recently learned that the city of Geneva has erected a statue in his honor.

[10]The provenance of the other texts in *Frontiers,* to the extent they have been successfully traced, is as follows:

III, "Rain on the Frontiers," and V, "Post No Bills," were both previously published in *Armful of April* and are reprinted here with a few minor editorial corrections.

IV, "Bridges" was published first in *Foretaste* in 1984, as the seventh part of a sequence called "Itinerary" which runs throughout that book.

X, "Meditation on the Frontier" and XI, "Distant Comedy" appear in *Men at Work,* identical to our versions. "Meditation" appeared previously in a catalogue for a Batuz exposition, "Project for Berlin" in 1984, translated there into German and English. "Distant Comedy" is one of the titles in "Windows on the Inner Landscape" accompanying photographic reproductions of Jĭří Kolář's collages/chiasmages in 1982. This text is discussed in the conversations and has become "Windows on the Inner Passage" in the Postscript. (There is fluctuation between "Window" and "Windows.")

XII, "Song of the Rose of Voices" might be an expansion on the "Madrigal of the Rose of Voices," a musical score by Henri Pousseur published in 1984. It is linked in the bibliography of *Frontiers* to the "Vision of Namur" and in the Postscript mentioned as a recording.

Other references within the texts include Butor's piece, "36 and 10 Views of Fuji," mentioned in the "53 Stages," which appears in *Repertory III.* "The Parliament of Idols," mentioned only in the Postscript, is one of the exposition catalogues for an exhibit "based on an idea of Butor's as realized by Maccheroni" in 1985. "Elseneur" also mentioned only in the Postscript, is a "dramatic suite" as proposed to the composer René Koering, the elements of which were developed by the artist Christian Dotrement and Butor by correspondence. This opera was broadcast on French National Radio in 1979. Koering had earlier written, in collaboration with Butor, "Listening Post," which was broadcast on radio in 1972, and two variants, "The Night Listens" and "Manhattan Invention." The latter was played and discussed at the Colloquium at Cerisy dedicated to Butor in 1974.

[11]Toru Shimizu describes this planned publication in detail, adding in a note that "due to financial reasons, the publication of this ideal bilingual version has been postponed for the moment" (*World Literature Today* 286).

[12]"Song of the Rose of Voices" probably contains citations from specific authors as well as their recognizable style and subject matter: a potentially fruitful subject for the Butor scholar.

Works Cited in the Introduction

(Essential Butor bibliography is contained in Part V.)

Baïche, André. *The Birth of the French Baroque: Poetry and Image, from the Pléiade to Jean de la Ceppède.* Toulouse: Associated Publishers of the University of Toulouse-le Mirail, 1976. Preface by Jacques Maurens.

Butor, Michel. "Meditation on the Frontier." Leon S. Roudiez, tr. *Project for Berlin.* Catalogue, Batuz exhibit. Koblenz: Görres-Drukerei and Co., 1984.

————. *Bicentennial Kit.* Paris: Philippe Lebaud, Le Club du Livre, 1975.

————. "Nine Classics of Japanese Art" (from *Floatings from East to West*), Terese Lyons, tr. *SubStance,* No. 33/34, X:4 (1981), 3-25.

————. "Forest Sounds," in *Patrice Pouperon.* Avignon: Mediathèque Municipale, 1984.

————. *The Parliament of the Idols.* Nice: Villa Arson, February-April, 1985.

————. *Windows on the Inner Landscape.* Reproductions of collages/chiasmages of Jiří Kolář. Bois-de-Champs: Aenerages & Co., 1982.

Koering, René. "A note: to be a musician and to collaborate with Butor." Georges Raillard, *Butor/Colloquium of Cerisy.* Paris: General Union of Publishers, 1974, 299-305.

Lydon, Mary. *Perpetuum Mobile: A Study of the Novels and Aesthetics of Michel Butor.* Edmonton, Alberta, Canada: University of Alberta Press, 1980.

McWilliams, Dean. "Butor's American Texts: The Writer as Red Indian." *World Literature Today,* No. 2 (Spring 1982), 286-91.

————. *The Narratives of Michel Butor: The Writer as Janus.* Athens, Ohio: Ohio University Press, 1978.

First Part
SITUATING

CRITICISM—WHETHER IT BE JOURNALISTIC OR EVEN, SOME-times, scholarly—has this bad habit of talking about books as if neither those who wrote them nor those who will read them had ever read anything.

Chaste silence. One would betray the author by revealing the names of those by whom he is inspired, those from whom he derives—and whom, on reading his work, no critic worthy of the name can fail to recognize.

The writer would be a creator, and all creation would be done necessarily *ex nihilo,* or rather *ex vita,* that is to say, on the basis of experience directly, immediately, authentically lived—because one would really live only what one saw somewhere other than in books, and only that would be worthy of giving rise to new books.

However, if one writes, it is exactly because one has first read! It is because one has loved at least some books madly! It is even because those books were no longer enough for us. Because they no longer sufficed to satisfy the taste they had aroused. Because they did not say everything, because certain elements of our own experience found no place there— whose importance, from that moment, as in a negative, appeared to us clearer and more distinct than ever. . . And it is also because in rereading them over and over, ever more closely, we believed we had discerned the crack (the passage) through which to introduce a little of what they lacked.

Unless—and I have certainly said as much—it is the readers who are taken for simpletons! They would be capable of reading Proust only through their taste for madeleines and flowering young girls; Dostoievsky through their passion for gambling. . . .

What a mistake! If we continue to read at an age, at a time, when nothing obliges us to any longer, it is certainly because we are curious to discover how a book can still be produced. It is through a taste for formal invention just as lively, just as strong, as the need we all feel to see the world we live in finally represented.

In a study dated 1955, Michel Butor wrote: *"It is clear that the world in which we live is being transformed with great speed. The traditional techniques of the story are incapable of integrating all the new relationships thus cropping up. A perpetual uneasiness results from this: it is impossible for us to organize in our consciousness all the information that assails it, because we lack adequate tools."*

And later: *"Formal invention in the novel, far from being opposed to realism, as short-sighted criticism too often imagines it, is the condition sine qua non of a deeper realism."*

Furthermore, to read well, we should be able to make use of some landmarks! Where is our place in the history of literature? We read in the papers entire pages on Butor, Sollers or Robbe-Grillet, but who will finally permit us to *situate* them? Who will tell us what problems each of these authors in his own way confronts? What then does his share of success and his share of defeat really consist of? What solution does each one propose for what difficulty and what better solution could be provided?

Michel Butor more than anyone else seemed to us aware of his place in a world already saturated with writing. It is he whom we went to question.

—Christian Jacomino

Second Part
CONVERSATIONS

I. EXTERIOR

Christian Jacomino: I'd like for us to talk about the exterior, the exteriors of Michel Butor, about your art as that of crossing the most spaces possible, of covering the greatest distances in the most foreign spaces, about your skillfulness and your obstinacy in inventing forms capable of integrating the largest possible number of things which until then had remained elusive, as if mad from wandering in outer space. But where to begin? I propose this: a parallel, an historical metaphor.

Michel Butor: It doesn't matter, my friend, provided we get going.

Ch. J.: Then let's try this way. . . . Specialists tell us how a revolution was brought about in the history of painting when, in the middle of the nineteenth century, first with Courbet and then with Manet and the Impressionists, painters left their studios to go work in the open air, in nature. Now, it is perhaps time to wonder if an analogous phenomenon did not occur, at about the same period, in literature, perhaps with Chateaubriand, then in a completely determined way with Nerval, and if this sudden sally did not have consequences just as decisive, just as lasting in the history of literature.

M. B.: Just the same, my impression is that it's fairly different. As to Courbet, we do know that he paints exteriors, but he does it like a landscape painter of the seventeenth century, that is, he goes outside to make sketches and then works up his painting at home, inside his studio, in the great *Studio of the Louvre*. It's later that painters (those of the Barbizon school) started taking walks with their paraphernalia and then installing themselves before the subject and finishing their painting on the spot. As to literature, the equivalent would be a writer who writes outside his office, who writes away from his individual work table.

Ch. J.: Isn't it in a café that we best picture Verlaine in the process of composing?

M. B.: Probably. There have been writers who work in cafés, I think, for a fairly long time. Even in the eighteenth century people worked, people wrote in a café, especially the journalists; they wrote in the evening right after leaving the theatre, for example. In the nineteenth century there were evidently people who wrote outside their own homes. But as for

Chateaubriand and Nerval, they did it for very precise reasons: it was because they were on a journey, and during their journey they took notes which would be thoroughly worked out only on their return. As for me, I write above all when I am settled somewhere. I need a place that is sufficiently "neutralized," which means perhaps that I am not really an outside writer. I bring back things to the inside of my burrow or my lair to work on, to absorb and transform. I am certainly a travel writer; I have traveled a lot and travel is one of the primary "sources" of my inspiration; but, up to now, I have written fairly little during the journey itself. Most of the time, I wait to be back in my habitual workplace to begin to compose and that even if the journey is relatively long.

I've taken trips which lasted a fairly long time, trips during which I gave lectures and where I moved around a lot, where I slept almost every night in a different place—well, during those trips, I wrote nothing; everything was stored away for the moment of my return; besides that, sometimes I had to wait weeks or months before being able to work on notes I'd taken and on the few documents I'd been able to accumulate. But also, I've happened to make fairly long stays in foreign countries, and in those cases I settled in, I had a second home. In those cases it was no longer just a journey; it was actually a move. The longest trip I took without returning to France was one of my trips to the United States; it lasted fourteen months. Then the trip I made to Berlin also lasted a little more than a year. In those two circumstances I had to settle down. I worked a great deal in the United States and I worked a great deal in Germany—but to do it, to begin to compose, to be able to fill up the blank pages, I needed to feel sufficiently trustful of the things that surrounded me, of the place. I needed to feel sufficiently at home, and that is why it took me about three weeks or a month to settle in. During the first month I was incapable of writing; after this period of taking possession, I could begin to bring to my new burrow a certain number of things. But everything has become complicated since then. As my journeys to foreign countries became steadily more numerous and longer, I've had to learn to adapt more quickly. Certain journeys have become very regular: I think especially of those to Geneva. Each week I commute between Geneva and Nice, and it's clearly necessary for me to feel settled there. But I reserve this Genevan time for my university work—it's in this way that I manage to balance, to organize my existence—and thus I work for myself, I really write, especially when I am here. But of course there are things which overflow. It can happen that, while I am in Geneva, I take some notes. It even happens that I write in the means of transportation, that is to say, I work in the train or plane. This is a completely recent phenomenon and I was totally unable to do this before, but I think (I hope) it will develop, because it is certainly one of my dreams to write while in motion.

When I was in the United States, when we were staying in the American West, we often saw those magnificent units on wheels passing by, those sorts of trailers they call *campers*. It would be like a dream for me to have a big trailer of that kind, inside which I'd be nicely settled and where I could type while the landscape changed. One can easily imagine a kind of network, modeled after service stations, but which would be made up of bookstores, libraries, archives, etc. One would stop from time to time to return worn out books and take out others. . . . That is what I would like, but, you see, when I wrote a book like *Description of San Marco,* I was very far from the site. I went to Venice, I collected, I photographed in my head or recorded a certain number of things. I identified a certain number of documents which could be useful to me, which could allow me to work out this description—and then I went home. At that time I think I must have been living at Sainte-Geneviève-des-Bois, in the southern suburbs of Paris. It is there that I wrote this entire description for which memory thus played a thoroughly essential role. And all that is just to say that my work seems to me to be related more to that of Courbet than to that of Claude Monet.

Ch. J.: You don't write or rarely, you say, outside. However, I continue to think that you're situated exactly at the forefront of an already old and increasingly violent movement which consists of making literature come forth from what I'd call its Great Reserves. But to make myself better understood, I'll have to seek my references at some distance. Let's look at Montaigne—you know him well and will tell me if I'm mistaken. We have his *Journal of a Voyage to Italy.* It isn't a misunderstood work at all, but you'll agree with me that it remains nonetheless marginal, that its importance is in no way comparable to that of the *Essays.* Let's now compare Montaigne's case to Chateaubriand's, two and one half centuries later, and what do we find? That in the work of Chateaubriand, a work just as central to the history of our literature, the journal, the travel story has become something like the center. Then we find Nerval—he is probably the turning-point. His journeys may be to very distant places, as are the "real journeys," or may take place only around Paris, and this shrinking appears to me to be of the greatest importance. Indeed, what justifies the keeping and the publication of a journal of a trip to the Orient is that the Orient remains unknown—it's thus original information that this writing can contain and bring to his reader—it's at least exoticism. But when the journey is limited to the surroundings of Paris, then this informational justification, this alibi of exoticism, no longer exists. The journal is no longer read for whatever novelty it might bring us, but as the illustration of a new literary genre, like a new model of literature. And isn't it exactly into this breach, this crack, this passage, that the Surrealists are going to rush? I am thinking, of course, of *Mad Love,* and *Peasant of Paris*. . . of so many of these little marvels of prose.

M. B.: There is, before Chateaubriand, a whole tradition of travel writers who, besides, are not sufficiently studied (for the Orient, I think of Tavernier, Chardin, etc.). And then, concerning Montaigne, I believe that his *Journal of a Voyage to Italy* is something very important, but it's true that its status remains rather special, because a great part of it was written by a secretary and not by Montaigne himself. As for Chateaubriand, obviously the journey plays an absolutely essential role. One can even say that his work is constructed by it: his two long journeys, on the one hand to America, toward the west, on the other hand to the Orient, *Itinerary from Paris to Jerusalem and from Jerusalem to Paris.* This one was written in a fairly complex way; these are travel stories rather than journals. There are, in some passages, notes which are presented as having been taken from day to day, and then there are others in which there is considerable perspective. Very often with the Romantics we witness this phenomenon: we have elements of a journal and then we have elements of stories, I would say travel memoirs, and we find that in Nerval. There are passages in the *Voyage to the Orient* which are presented as a journal; there are others where it's no longer a question of that at all, where it's the author, returned home, who studies, who works on the basis of his memories, and who even invents. The true travel journals we'll find in Gide—for example, the *Voyage to the Congo.* But with the great Romantics, we have evidently an essential presence of travel, with text written while traveling, but especially (and this is what you wanted to get at) one sees travel become a theme, or even more, something like a model; thus, when one is at home, it's in order to travel again, and that not only in a metaphorical way.

It's not only a question of interior travel, but to profit truly from the trip one has taken. One settles down at home to work on this trip, which will permit one to prepare later trips. And this very important idea, thoroughly decisive, of the intimate link between travel and literature, is something which Romanticism (English and German before French) has bequeathed us. It is something which it emphasized, there is no doubt about that. To be very clear, it was absolutely necessary that there be great journeys. For Chateaubriand, with the East and West, he extends as far as possible the scope of his own breathing. One could say that other directions are still lacking, the North and South, which are directions literature has not much explored even since then. It was especially the journey to the East that was explored by the literature of the nineteenth century, until Barrès and Gide. The journey to the West, the journey toward the United States, was explored by some authors in the nineteenth century, but very rarely—the most important being Tocqueville—and then there are some traces, here or there, but the dissymmetry is remarkable. It's in the twentieth, even the second half of the century, that the journey to America has become so important in French literature. For that it was necessary that things be very obvious, it was necessary to be able to rely on those predecessors: for the Romantics, to go to Cairo, to go to Constantinople, was going almost as far as possible; the rest was so far away as to be no longer distinguishable.

The last great romantic journey to the East, I think, was Flaubert's. At the beginning he wanted to take a longer trip with Maxime du Camp than the one he actually took. He intended to go to Bagdad and even as far as Persia; and then the funds began to give out, and when they were in Beirut, Jerusalem, Constantinople, they decided that that was enough, that they had gone as far as the others. They covered almost the same Orient as the others, with however a detour toward the south. Whereas neither Chateaubriand nor Nerval had gone south of Cairo, Flaubert and Maxime du Camp went down to Ouadi Halfa, that is to say, to the present frontier of Sudan. Thus they went farther south than the others; they extended somewhat the journey to the Orient of the great Romantics. But, what is important to us is that once the journey to the Orient was accomplished, well, any moving around then in the interior of Europe at all could be in some way representative of it.

There already is a great Romantic, a great travel enthusiast, who never went to the Orient, who is Victor Hugo. He replaced the journey to the Orient with the journey to Germany. And for him, the equivalent of the journey to America was obviously the exile in the Anglo-Norman islands. . . . In his book on the Rhine, he even says, "Germany is the Indies of the West," and it is true that one can take trips which are images of miniatures of other trips—thus trips to the interior of France. In the case of Nerval, to be sure, his walks in the Parisian region became equivalents of the journey to the Orient and are illuminated by it. . . . But let me return to Flaubert. Before going to the Orient he had already taken some trips which were fairly long for the period. When he was very young (after having passed his baccalaureate exam, I think) his parents offered him a trip to the Pyrenees and to Corsica. He had to cross the sea and that was already an extraordinary adventure. And then, he accompanied his sister on a wedding journey a little while later, to Rome; next, already in the company of Maxime du Camp, he traveled the Loire valley, Brittany and Normandy. There is a preface in which he says that another time, later if he can, he will go to the Orient, and the Orient of the Romantics included even Andalusia, the western province of cultures centered at Constantinople, Bagdad, Cairo, etc. Thus, this trip to Brittany and Normandy represents a substitute for the journey to the Orient. . . . You see, within smaller and smaller regions we can thus have substitute journeys, and the moving about of the author (or of his characters or or his preoccupations) will play an essential role, informed as he is by moments of the great journeys that he has been able to experience. And in this regard, it is true that I situate myself altogether in the tradition of these Romantic writers. That is to say that the great journeys I have made illuminate even my little changes of place. When I take a walk, if only here on the Mont Boron, there are instances when a light, a tree, remind me of something I have seen in Egypt, that I have seen in the United States or that I have seen in Japan, in such a way that the world begins to turn under my feet. The Earth turns when I take a walk, and the Earth certainly turns when I am at my table and I write.

II. NAVIGATION

Ch. J.: When asked, and you did it again at the time of our previous meeting, you have very often told people, "I take very few notes when I am traveling." But at other times, in a completely parallel sense, it has occurred to you to compare literary work—and there, I think that you were thinking of the work of the reader as well as that of the writer—to a sort of navigation. It's impossible to read your work, and even to hear you, without experiencing a sort of vertigo: you seem to me to have a completely *oceanic* vision, conception, of literature. . . . But I must be precise. . . . You've explained to us in what way you were able to compose the *Description of San Marco;* you said: "I did not take notes at the site, I committed to memory what could be useful to me and also, and especially, I helped myself to documents at the site, to bring home and work on afterwards." I believe this is, indeed, a way of proceeding which is very familiar to you, very habitual: you do not take notes at the site but you tear away from that site something which, in a certain way, is an intimate part of it, a little like those painters who could not go walking without collecting stones, roots, pieces of Nature to bring home to their studio. But in the case of a writer, what does that mean? Well, it signifies that, for you, one doesn't write in a void, not starting from nothing, from silence, from a blank, on that empty page which the blankness of Mallarmé protects but rather on the bottom of an ocean of spoken and written discourse, spoken by everyone and written for a utilitarian purpose, not expressly literary at all, on which you'll have to navigate, on which you'll have to make your way in order not to drown, which—willy-nilly—you'll have to use. . . . With you (and with some others before you whom we will have to discuss) it's no longer so much to produce discourse as to make use, to put into form, the ocean of discourse which precedes us all.

Thus I notice that when one opens the first volume of your *Repertory* (I recall that there are five) and then chooses the very first study in this first volume, one can read this from the first line: *The novel is a particular form of story. This latter is a phenomenon which extends considerably beyond the domain of literature: it is one of the essential components of our apprehension of reality. Until our death, and from the time we have understood speech, we are perpetually surrounded by stories, first of all in our family, then in school, then through meetings and readings. Others, for us, are not only what we have seen with our own eyes, but what they have told us about themselves, or what others have told us about them. They are not only those whom we have seen, but also all those about whom people have told us. This is not only true of men, but of things themselves, places, for example, where I have not gone, but which have been described to me. This story in which we are steeped takes the most varied forms....* There, I could continue, adding to the number of quotations. When discussing literary work is the issue, you begin by making reference to this oceanic background of language which goes beyond you, which transcends you on all sides.

M. B.: I believe, indeed, that it's very important. But it's not only characteristic of my own literary work: all literature proceeds from that. What characterizes my work is perhaps that I realize this inescapable reality, that I realize that one writes always inside something, that one writes against a background that is already given, with materials which already exist. If I proceed thus, I am evidently not the only one to do so. I do it perhaps differently because there is an awareness on my part which does not exist in certain others. Thus, it is absolutely certain that when I travel I am not only a spectator and a listener, I am also a reader of the landscape. When I travel in a country, I am going to read books concerning it, but it is especially to help me read the country itself. And I am going to listen to what people say, I am going to look at the texts that are found there, which constitute this background on which other words appear, detach themselves—these texts which are, some of them, literary, but very often also related to the law, to advertising, to all sorts of utilitarian ends, some fragments of which I'll try to take home, samples, to be able to subject them later to analyses, to make them react with other kinds of materials, and so forth.... When I travel in a country, from the beginning I am looking for what I could say about it and how to do it. But there are numerous countries where I've been and of which I haven't yet spoken and of which perhaps I'll never speak; it isn't that they are less beautiful than the others, it is simply that I haven't yet found the means, the form I am seeking. There are some for which it has taken me a long time; I've had to go back there. There are some which struck me at first with such a strangeness that I had the impression that I would never be able to talk about them, or that perhaps I would talk about them, but that it was impossible for me to say anything interesting about them immediately. I had to go further, I had to tame this country, to become capable of receiving its teaching; for it's the country itself which teaches us how we can speak of it. Obviously there are some things I see immediately. Often, when I am traveling, I say to myself, "Look! There is something there." I feel there is the starting point of a text for me, the start of a book. I say to myself, "Look! That, that ought to work." But when this feeling of a click occurs, I don't even need to note it down, because it occurs strongly enough to be able to organize things around it, and around a certain number of clefts of the same sort; and consequently I'm certain I can find it again.

Sometimes there's this impression that reality is opening up, is beginning to speak. Sometimes it's about to fade away; sometimes I don't succeed in responding to this call given to me; then it's because there was something illusory, or that remained illusory for a very long time. It can happen that what did not manage to take shape for years becomes, thanks to other encounters, finally usable. But when these moments occur, which are so important for me, I don't feel the need to write them down immediately, and even mistrust immediate notation. This is because this feeling indicates to me that something is in the process of beginning, that I'm beginning to understand something, but am only at the very first babblings. That leads me to seek information here and there, and it's only when I have obtained this information that I become capable of speaking, of explaining a bit what happened, of understanding what this feeling of things opening meant. And it's somewhat the same phenomenon which occurs in the course of my explorations in literature.

When I give a course on a writer, I'm obliged to reread that author as completely as possible. I will reread him several times, which implies that I won't be able to talk about everything. There are moments when I say to myself, "Look! There's something which has not yet really been said, something which people haven't seen and to which I could draw attention. There's something I'm going to be able to say which will make my course original, new, which will justify it in some way." Well, that appears at the turning of a page; then I could immediately note the sentence which struck me, but in general I don't unless I'm very late, unless the course or the composition of the essay is going to be due very soon. I don't, because I let it work in the interior of my memory; it had to travel to the interior of myself. Several times I've been able to verify that, when I took notes too quickly, well, I missed the very things I find most interesting. Whenever I read, there's always a moment when I say to myself, "Here is something new, essential!" and then I reflect and I begin to give a little structure to my course or my essay, and then I know the whole of the text well enough to be able to find the quotations again that I'll need, and when the time comes for me to look for those quotations again, those which struck me to begin with, I have to descend again into the interior of the text—and it has very often happened that I discover that what was most significant was not the passage I'd noticed, but something two pages earlier or two pages later. It's something, certainly, which is linked, which corresponds to the place which called out to me, but elsewhere it is clearer still.

The best essays I've been able to do are those I worked on in that fashion, which requires, of course, that time not be too meagerly allotted, because it requires one more reading, and still one more reading, and so on. When I teach my courses, obviously my quotations must be noted, immediately accessible and available; therefore, at that time, but only at that time, I slip bookmarks inside the book I'm using. It's very convenient, but one must recognize that things are then fixed fast. It happens that I draw a text from a course I have taught (such as, recently, the one on Flaubert) but then I can't add any quotations, only take them away. It's not the time to rummage about. . . . You understand! Leaving things supple and mobile long enough is very precious to me.

And what is true for travels through literature is also true for travels in the real world. There are trips taken in order to extract a book from them, planned with that in mind. Then I'll open my eyes and strain my ears in an altogether special way. I look for things of a certain type, those that can go into the book that is already beginning to write itself, that, in my head at least, is already clearly organized. But within this categorization, this range, it's very important that things remain flexible enough for something new to happen. What comes to me as new is what I can give to others that is most new; I have experienced that many times. The documents I bring back, the prospectuses, the texts of all kinds which I discover at the sites, the Art books, that all weighs very heavy. Around that, things will be organized in a fairly requisite fashion. But for all of that, it's not yet fixed in what I'd call the glue, the cement of writing. There's a certain play still, and I'll maintain this play until the end, until the moment when I compose the text itself.

Ch. J.: Yes, I think here we are reaching a characterization of your procedure which is both very precise and altogether impressive. I say impressive because when you spoke of your delay in noting down what will be most useful to you in a text, I thought that the quality that would be most indispensable to you would be not the strength of the divine Achilles nor that of René Char, but rather the prudence and guile of old Ulysses, the composure of a ship's captain like Nemo or of some other Jules Verne hero. Indeed, you must be capable of seeing danger (the end, the due date) as it comes, and of still putting off as long as possible the decision-making moment. You see that I'm sticking to my oceanic metaphor—and for good reason. I mentioned Mallarmé, but we should speak of Francis Ponge. The latter—whom I know you esteem very highly and to whom you appear to be very similar in some respects—accumulates notes, but in such a way that one always has the feeling that he begins to write before having the slightest idea, before having decided on any sense of direction, black on white, whereas you say, "I read an author (or, just as well a Japanese landscape) and I'm waiting to discover something like a possible starting point there, what others haven't seen, that is to say, a hole, a gap, a crack, a slip." In the density of this world which is so noisy with language, you seek a passage to make your way. And I believe something very new in literature is there, perhaps the very mark of modernity. Apollinaire and Proust, Joyce probably, did not remain deaf to this rustling of the world. You have studied them a great deal. But what gives promise in them becomes, with you, systematic. I don't see any equivalent, in our language at least, except Denis Roche, and besides I believe both of you would be better understood if people thought—I mean professional critics, academics, those whose profession it is—to consider you two together more often. Shouldn't we also extend the observation to the other Arts of our time? Thus, what have musicians done? They, too, have discovered that the world isn't mute, that it's thus not so much a question of producing sounds as of treating those that surround us, to render them distinct, "possible" (as Ponge would say), that is, acceptable to us. And so even with the plastic Arts. . . .

But before going too far in this direction, I'd like to point out how all this is closely related to the theme of travel: as long as the artist remains at home, he neither sees nor hears anything of what surrounds him. He thus has to invent. But in going out, in distancing himself from that famous, supposedly ivory tower, he discovers that nothing in the nature of the world is completely indifferent, and on his return, his very room, his "library," can seem to him richer than Ali Baba's cave. He discovers that everything is there, that he only needs to bend down—which means perhaps: finally to show humility.

M. B.: In this regard it's indeed a question of the reversal of a certain number of thoroughly fundamental notions, of something therefore like a revolution. . . . You speak of the blank page and the vertigo of the blank page and indeed, for a long time, perhaps for always, the writer was someone who had the feeling of adding something; the background of texts was thin and the role of the writer was to add to it. In the same way, for a long time musicians believed that there was silence and that their role was to add sound, noise to it. . . . It is a phenomenon which is still established elsewhere, on a whole different scale of values. Thus, for a long time, an improved lot was worth more than a vacant lot, but when all the space is already occupied, then the vacant lot appears the more valuable. Look at the interior of Manhattan Island, especially around Wall Street: what's worth the most and assumes the most prestige is emptiness. A lot which isn't improved is more valuable than another because what might be on it doesn't have to be demolished, and when one is able to leave some emptiness, to set aside a little square for the neighborhood, a little open space, then that is the truest sign of wealth. For a long time the sign of wealth was to construct taller and taller skyscrapers, but we have reached the point that there are so many very tall skyscrapers that what is stronger than a still taller skyscraper is the absence of any building. To succeed in setting aside open space in the middle of those towers is something extraordinary.

Today's musicians have become more and more vividly aware that silence is something willed, constructed, obtained, that it's exactly that which music provides. And that's a very important change relative to classic sensitivity or that of the beginning of romanticism. A statement like Pascal's famous one, "The silence of these infinite spaces frightens me. . ." does not have for us the same resonance at all that it could have had for our ancestors, because today even a child knows that those supposedly "infinite" spaces (I mean that the concept itself no longer has the same meaning for us as for Pascal), that these infinite spaces are actually full of noises. We spend our time listening to them and we know very well that, when the quantity of sounds is diminished as far as possible, when we find ourselves in an echo-free room to make acoustical experiments, we feel a sort of vertigo, because the sonorous presence of the world is placed in parentheses, vanishes. It's a very curious phenomenon. One has a troubling sensation which can even extend to a loss of equilibrium, but there are the internal noises of the body which acquire at this point an extreme importance. It's the most dazzling demonstration that we are in nature, that we are a part of it, that, most often, we don't perceive our own sounds simply because the sounds of the world come cover them up. When we suppress the sounds of the world, then our own music fills the space. . . . And musicians know now that their art does not consist only in filling silence, that a concert is also silence. It is a ceremony whose sonata, which the concert offers, is actually only a "piece," a part. There is a critical moment when the conductor arrives, the moment when he raises his baton and everyone falls silent. . . . Any radio technician knows that silences always have a color, which is why when they interview people and want to make montages afterwards, they take care to record silence. Otherwise the ear would very easily perceive the moment when the change took place. There is suddenly something which the listener is incapable of analyzing but which will disturb him considerably.

  Ch. J.: The sounds of the world. . . . I think of Proust, of course, waking up and the sounds of the street reaching his ear, sounds of those little trades now vanished. And I wonder if the perception of certain sounds (their new "eminence") doesn't correspond to a sudden awareness of what they express, of what they give evidence of. . . . Could one notice what seemed to be without any merit? Unquestionably, to attribute merit to something it is necessary to notice it; but I wonder if this proposition cannot be, ought not to be reversed. In other words, if the artist has considered for a long time that the world was silent, was it because he didn't hear it or rather because, for him, the sounds of the world, those produced by the "tradespeople," each and every one, were devoid of all value?

  M. B.: Since the sixteenth century there have been people like Clément Jannequin or Orlando Gibbons listening to the cries of Paris or London. But we've been led to listen to them much more closely, and these sounds have begun to speak to us as they never did before. Just as when I read a text, there is a moment when I say to myself, "Well, there's something which hasn't been seen," in the same way the musician began, little by little, to listen to environmental sounds, saying to himself, "There, with that things could be made which have not yet been made," and in the same way the painter, who was walking in the fields, one fine day said to himself, "Why there is enough here to make a Ruysdael that would be better than a Ruysdael. There is a Claude Lorrain of there is an anti-Claude Lorrain. There is enough to bring a certain newness to our repertory." But I'd like to come back to that story of the blank page. . . .

For a long time, the page remained blank and the problem was to know what to put on it; whereas for many of us today it is the reverse. The page is not blank; the page is already all covered with texts; the world is covered with texts and this blankness is a little like the silence fabricated by the musician, a space which one arranges artificially in order to be able to intervene there in a way which is our own. I mean that the blank page is something like a metaphor of this open space that we try to introduce everywhere, in a world which appears to be already saturated. Certainly there are still regions of reality which are like deserts; there are even regions which are practically unknown, but there are fewer and fewer of them. Remember that moment in the history of the United States. . . .

It was in the nineteenth century that what they call the "frontier" disappeared. The history of the United States begins with the thirteen colonies on the Atlantic Coast. Little by little they will reach toward the West, and the feeling that one has that it's always possible to stretch out in that direction, well! It allows for great optimism, extraordinary breathing room. All things are possible, because one always has the feeling that there will be space ahead. What they call the "frontier" is not then the boundary between two almost similar regions, but that between a region which is fairly full and another which is considered (perceived) as relatively empty— although this emptiness is as inhabited as our silence, because they will find Indians there, buffalo and many other things besides. But it is perceived as a reserve, in the most general sense; they will be able to stretch out indefinitely. All things are possible because they are expanding, because they still have so much room at their disposal that nothing will be able to stop us. And then the colonists settled on the West Coast and we will witness a series of Gold Rushes which will, little by little, allow the establishment of a whole network of communications on these lands which are no longer wild. And there is a very important moment when the two waves will meet and when there will be no more "frontier" in the traditional sense (one should say almost legendary) of the American nineteenth century. Because, from that moment on, in spite of the enormous unfilled spaces not ruled off in grids, which remain in American space, there is something which ends; the very condition of American existence is transformed. It is remarkable: there's a moment when they know that all the space has been occupied. There are places which are still almost empty, but they know that it's a matter of a few years, and problems are already presented in a completely different way. And what's true for the United States can be generalized. . . .

There's first the invention of big cities, which coincides with other phenomena of great importance, like the appearance of writing. The latter brings about an enormous change in human behavior, because, since that time we have lived in the same opposition of city-country. . . . It's the generative principle of the Roman Empire, always reactivated by the papal benediction: "urbi et orbi. . . ." But now today we witness almost everywhere in the world the following phenomenon: urban centers have developed so vigorously, cities are so stretched out that their limits meet. There is no longer a background of countryside in the middle of a reality which is fundamentally urban, or, more precisely, suburban, because there is no longer one center, there is no longer anything but suburbs. We can say that our time is that of the generalization of suburbs, with centers, no doubt, but which are always relative. We had cities in the middle of the country; we now have country in the middle of the city. . . . And in the same way in literature, libraries are already full. It is evident for everyone that we cannot read everything which has been written, that we cannot even read everything which is recognized as a masterpiece. We do not have the time. . . . As a result, when we write we do not interpose on the blankness. The blankness is something which we are going to use to interpose, to emphasize certain elements of what is already written.

It is impossible not to know that libraries are more and more numerous and better and better equipped, and that all sorts of new techniques let us make many copies of the text and study it differently. And it is the same thing with images. A painting formerly was something which one added to a non-pictorial reality that constituted the background; whereas now, images superimpose themselves on reality. Formerly one knew that such and such a painting was held in such and such a private collection or in such and such a museum, and to see it one had to go there. Whereas now any painting at all is found at the source of an army of reproductions which invade all the aspects of our daily life. Whether we like it or not, the Mona Lisa is everywhere.

Ch. J.: From which the keynote so characteristic of our era—of constant renewal, of originality, of newness at any price. When the Renaissance painter received an order from the Prince, his first concern was to make something which would satisfy this patron, which corresponded to his tastes and his convictions. It mattered little to this Prince, and thus little also to the painter, that the same subject had been treated in about the same way on the walls of another palace, in another city some hundreds of miles away. These two frescos would never be brought face to face, juxtaposed, except in the memory of a very small number of travelers; one cannot take the place of the other. But when all the frescos, all the altar pieces, and all the paintings ever painted can be found everywhere, accessible to everyone, thanks to the reproductions that have been made of them, then the artists, before worrying about pleasing whoever it might be, must ask themselves, "What can I make that does not yet exist? What can I make that is different, new, that at least some difference, some newness justifies?" I mean that today each painting adds itself to and thus must justify itself in relation to the total number of those produced since the beginning of time. I mean that the talent of the painter is no longer that of producing something true or beautiful, which would justify itself, but rather that of intervening in a necessarily original way in the space of the universal art gallery.

M. B.: And to find its place in this art gallery, it must necessarily disturb or perhaps even eliminate one or more of the paintings already there. . . . Having said this, I must add that we should certainly not imagine that today only novelty is produced. Absolutely not! We find ourselves in a situation where the works which already exist are multiplied indefinitely, thanks to more or less faithful reproductions, and it's more and more necessary to open a window in the space on this wall which is perpetually thickening. One can say that if for yesterday's writer it was a question of adding something, well, today the question is that of starting with an extremely loud background noise, which must be dug into thoroughly to discover, rediscover things. . . . You remarked just now that when I am concerned with classic literature the most important moment is the one when, turning a page, I say to myself, "There's something that hasn't been seen before." This means that the book itself appears through a thickness of readings which have already been made. *Madame Bovary,*

Remembrance of Things Past, or else the *Essays* of Montaigne, no matter what classic work of art, has been covered over, saturated by readings made before me. And each time I must find the means to draw aside, to tear away this veil of previous readings. In most cases, I'll accept the traditional reading, continue in it, and it won't bother me because I myself am a creature of habit. But probably at a certain moment I'll perceive the possibility of drawing the veil aside and thus of discovering something new. I sense the possibility of showing in what way these former readings made a veil. There was something that wasn't seen, which until then remained hidden, and I sense the possibility of a revelation, of a liberation of the text itself. And what's true for reading is true for writing also. . . . Having said this, I must add that there are within this veil of readings made by others before me some very interesting things, and it is, of course, by using them as a starting point that I'm able to examine the text in order to find something new in it. I need this thickness produced by History, but I need also to cut windows in it to be able to breathe. That's why you can verify that, in this room where I work, I've left two walls empty of books. I write with books behind my back, to be pushed by them, but I need to have a window in front of me, to see the world and to be able to breathe.

III. ATTENTION

Ch. J.: In a conversation with Roger Borderie, published as preface to your *Approach Works*, you say: *"What distinguishes me the most from the Surrealists in appearance, is the interest I have, unlike most of them, in a certain form of daily banality which is, however, admirably felt in the great biographical texts of Breton. Thus, samples of letters in the 'Project Blues,' certainly fictitious, are given as raw materials: they could have been cut out, torn out of a real correspondence. This intervention of what is written every day outside any idea of a literary work is very complex and touches a fundamental point. I absolutely refuse to eliminate a part of reality, to reject it as not being worth the trouble to bother with. In my poetry, even in that which is closest to Surrealism, there is this down-to-earth side which the Surrealists often evaded. But I must immediately amend what I just said by underscoring that it is to a large extent in the Surrealists and the people who surrounded them that I found the seeds of such a realism."*

This is a text which seems very important to me, not only to situate you, but to understand all the history of contemporary literature. You situate yourself relative to Surrealism in a completely contradictory way but, however contradictory, it seems to me the only pertinent one. I'm aiming at the idea here, the notion of "value" which I resorted to in our previous conversation. . . . And we noted that the same promotion of the everyday is found in most other attempts of modern art. But now I wonder if we can't go further, examining the actual community which may exist between these different artistic approaches and certain of the most prominent theories of our century. I'm thinking, of course, of Marxism and psychoanalysis. Indeed, if we're told that Freud discovered the Unconscious—whose existence, it seems to me, had been felt long before him—didn't he discover something still more important—that is, that the words of the suffering individuals—not what is found hidden somewhere in their head, but rather those they utter, those they say, even when those words seem completely senseless—deserve to be listened to, are *worth* the attention of the one claiming to cure?

M. B.: Yes. However, in psychoanalysis there remains a rigid barrier between the therapist's speech, which little by little will bring the truth, and the patient's, in which there are, certainly, elements which are interesting, but whose interest remains hidden to the one who utters them. In the art of the twentieth century there is a whole evolution, a sort of "dialecticisation" of the frontier between the professional and his client. In the nineteenth century we have the Italian theatre, with the strongest possible frontier between those on the stage and those seated in the audience. The classical concert functions with this same gulf: there are those who make the music and those who listen; no mingling is wanted. And this barrier will be strengthened still further with the cinema. In the Italian theatre hall, a certain dialogue can still be established between the stage and the audience, but in the case of the cinema, the actors on the screen no longer risk being bothered by audience noise or demonstrations. They absolutely cannot reply. They know nothing about such things.

Ch. J.: Isn't it true as well that the cinema constitutes a very expensive, very heavy industry—hence the creation of fetiches, the star system. I can still say to myself on leaving a theatre, "Well! Why couldn't I try to put on a little show like that? I would be perfectly capable and it would be fun." Whereas the film spectator knows that he will never be a director and that he has little chance of having a career in Hollywood where these shows are produced. I mean that the places themselves are distant, mysterious, like the fabulous fortunes of those who succeed in this profession.

M. B.: Yes, we have in nineteenth-century art frontiers which are strongly marked and which in many cases have been further strengthened in the course of this century. . . . And let's note that they are not specific to art, that they are marked out in all sorts of other fields, in particular in medicine. The doctor, custodian of knowledge, proposes to cure a patient provided that the latter be willing to submit himself to him. The speech of the patient is considered as symptomatic speech, stamped with the seal of illusion, whereas that of the doctor is therapeutic speech, a speech thus of truth. The difference is irreducible and if Freud discovered the usefulness of listening to the patient in a much more attentive manner, it remains no less true that the patient's speech and the specialist's do not have the same value.

Ch. J.: The patient then does not always tell the truth, as Jacques Lacan—he at least—claims to do?

M. B.: No, for the psychoanalyst the patient does not always tell the truth even if there is always truth to be drawn from what he says. No, let me emphasize, in the eyes of the analyst he's incapable of it, if not because he's sick then because he's not a professional. Doctors ask you to describe the symptoms you feel, which is very difficult, which you're incapable of just as the doctor himself would be incapable. He knows that in all you say the largest part is to be rejected, that it constitutes only awkward padding, and Freud discovered the necessity of listening to absolutely everything the patient says, even what seems the most insane, but it's nonetheless true that what the patient says is always suspect, that his self-awareness can only be false. Everything must be said, but it must still be interpreted, and that can only be done by a specialist. . . . And it's very evident that, against this attitude, against this very strong frontier between doctor and patient, which still exists in psychoanalysis, all contemporary art rebels. In spite of all the uses artists and critics have been able to make of certain psychoanalytical notions, a distance has always been maintained— because psychoanalysis still, as it is currently practiced, remains a nineteenth-century medical art. It marks this frontier in an unequivocal way, in a rigid and absolute fashion.

This isn't to say that all things are so significant or that they would be significant in the same way. . . . When we say that the sounds of the world are beautiful, we do not mean that for us they all are equally so, in the same way. . . . Certain ones are better able to reveal the others to us, and the musician is the one who allows us to hear what is beautiful there where we were incapable of recognizing it before. It isn't a question of saying that the spectacle of the world is uniformly beautiful and that just anything has the same value as such and such a painting in the Louvre. It's a question of saying that the world proposes to us things which could give rise to paintings which have never been done and which will be just as significant.

Ch. J.: When artists cut from reality a parcel which they offer up to be seen, to be decoded by the whole of their reading public, they make a bet that this thing presents a meaning accessible to all, a universal value. Whereas, if I follow you correctly, in the case of the symptomatic words, they would be meaningful only in relation to the very individual experience of the patient. It would be useless to reproduce them, to make them known to others. They are presumably subject to interpretation, and this interpretation could effect the cure of the sufferer. But there could be no question of publishing, broadcasting, proposing these words to everyone, of making everyday expressions out of them.

M. B.: Just so. The science of medicine entirely dominates the words of the patient, whereas these words ought, in turn, to be able to transform the speech of the doctor himself. . . . You spoke of the artist who cuts something from the interior of reality and, indeed, it often happens that we use this process, which is found at the very heart of photography, because the latter consists above all of framing. It is an art of framing, thus of découpage. Whatever, through it, is caught, framed, cut out, perhaps inserted and further, treated according to more of less sophisticated techniques, can be offered up as something on the contrary completely raw, immediate. . . . And one finds the same concerns in many other domains of twentieth-century art.

It is the collage procedure, in the paintings of Braque or of Picasso, for example. . . . Instead of representing the thing by means of painting, they took the thing itself and glued it on the canvas. This could be a piece of newspaper, a subway ticket, or even a little sand. In this case we're dealing with a fragment of reality which claims to be as raw as possible. Of course, this immediacy is only relative. The choice and découpage of the piece of newspaper, the way in which it's glued on the canvas, all that transforms if considerably. It's a matter of a myth of immediacy, of a reference, of homage, of an ideal perhaps. . . . And in literature there may be all sorts of elements which play this role. One thinks of Apollinaire, of course, but one would find even in Balzac collage processes completely analogous to those of cubist painting. And I have worked a great deal on it myself. . . .

From all my travels, I've brought back snatches, I've brought back quotations. For the literary critic, it's a completely ordinary process since it is mandatory. For him it's a question of talking about an author and at the same time giving excerpts by the author himself to be read. On the same page, there'll be a text about Flaubert *and* the text by Flaubert himself, a little like the piece of newspaper in the cubist paintings. But what one must note well, that on which all our experimental work has focused, is the passage from one to the other, on all the possible degrees of integration. In all the fields which we have just passed in review, we must note that one evolves from a moment when things were considered as very clear-cut—with this absolute distinction between blank page and writing, between silence and sound, between doctor and patient, between representation and thing itself—to another moment when these distinctions, these limits, these frontiers, unravel and fade away, when everything communicates, without, for all that, intermingling.

Ch. J.: Absolutely! Let's think of *Boomerang,* of the four volumes of *Stuff of Dreams,* or of any one of your latest works. The reader is lost in them. Even if he is experienced, and has been reading and rereading you for a long time, it is almost impossible for him to recognize and distinguish what is yours and what comes from elsewhere. We're no longer within the logic of a random snip of the scissors at all—I mean, in a logic which could be that of the surrealists. With them, collage appears always like something daring, almost heroic, but at the same time a little mechanical. I am scarcely criticizing them. . . . It's really they who taught us to weigh the charms, the poetry of the mechanical, of the machine—see the superb illustrations of Max Ernst, for example. . . . But, indeed, in your latest works, one progresses to a completely different aesthetic. . . . You no longer play on the plastic qualities of the well-marked contrast, but on something else which I would call speed. The text quoted, used, seems to produce extremely fast flash effects, to the point of becoming scarcely perceptible. The whole is made to rotate like a kind of flying saucer, entirely elusive, at a vertiginous speed. . . .

M. B.: That's exactly what has preoccupied me. . . . We must recall that I am both a writer—"avant-garde" or "research" writer, as they say—*and* a professor. It's a double life which no doubt creates many problems, but which also presents certain advantages. The work of the literary critic has been very important for the production of my other books. I even think that has been more and more the case with time and that it's not just by chance if the books you mention were written while I was a university professor. . . .

I've had a fairly complicated career as a teacher. There are certainly periods in which I've done almost nothing but write. But for quite a few years I've had a teaching position which has become more and more demanding, and it's certain that this teaching has had a great deal of influence on what was going on in my books. . . . Thus, we were talking about the use of the quotation within works of literary criticism. There is the text of the critic himself and, set into that, there's the text of the author he is studying. In general the limit between the two is well marked, physically, visually emphasized by whatever kind of typographical procedure there may be. The quotations are a few lines extracted from their context, that is, from the milieu, from the element within which they made sense. The critic uses them to illustrate what he's proposing and therefore they take on a new sense in a new context. But that isn't enough. It's still important that these lines keep something of the freshness, of the life that could be theirs in the initial context. One too often sees quotations which are like dried flowers, whereas in the best critics these specimens stay alive. One studies them "in vivo" and not "in vitro. . . ." Well, this art of découpage is a very difficult thing, for which one must train a very long time, but the stakes are high! Indeed if the circulation (let's think of something like blood circulation) is maintained between the quotation and its original context, the reader of the article, the study, will probably want to go plunge into the work—and that is, of course, the purpose the work of the critic ought to serve. To get back to the books to which you refer, my concern has been to go further still than in my works of literary criticism. I wanted all I had been able to glean, here and there, to remain alive, but furthermore, I wanted the relations between my own text and all the quotations to become complex. I wanted the relations between quoted text and quoting text to be able to reverse themselves, the relationships not necessarily remaining stable. Thus in *Boomerang* I used texts from all sources and I confronted them with each other in such a way that they could quote or cite each other mutually. I use the word "cite" here in its judicial sense, that is, to accuse, to unmask, to reveal each other mutually.

Ch. J.: Between the original text and the quoted text, we should still mention the transitions, bridges, which you arrange, thanks mainly to the procedures of pastiche or parody.

M. B.: There are elements which I've collected and others I've had to create myself. But it's true that between the two there are all sorts of transitions. You speak of pastiches, parodies; these are procedures for which I have a predilection. But we should especially mention translations. These books are full of them. . . . If you translate an English text, for example, which is a little old, you can either modernize it or else attempt to keep its period character. You can try to make understood as rapidly as possible what the author wanted to say, but you can also make the text appear to the French reader today as the original would have appeared to its English readers, with the same time lag, and in this case you can amuse yourself by parodying the French of centuries past. And then a translation can be faithful to different degrees; it is like a quotation. . . . You see what happens when a quotation is concentrated through the deletion of certain words or fragments of sentences! You read a text which you could have read elsewhere, which you have perhaps already read, which you know—but you find yourself forced to read it more quickly or more slowly, with different scansions. It is an anamorphosis! And then when one writes a novel, one makes the characters talk, and the good novelist will be the one capable of inventing a different language for each character, to such an extent that the reader will have the impression of hearing the character himself speak and not the author of the novel. . . . And in the midst of all that, my own text will circulate in such a way that the quotations will find themselves in some way absorbed, incorporated into it. This is a matter of realizing a myth, a terribly deep and at the same time very poetic desire: that of becoming the other, of transforming oneself into and through the other. . . . Because, as a result of incorporating other texts into my text, even very celebrated authors, what happens is that my own identity is lost, that my own name will be inscribed within another name. . . .

Ch. J.: In listening to you, I think of a little text, quite recent, called *Distant Comedy,* where we find again the principal characters of the theatre of Molière, where we cross the whole universe of this author but at high speed and rather as in a dream. I mean that this universe which you describe, or rather which you reconstitute with the greatest detail, is that of Molière—no doubt about it, but for all that, it's not that of any one of his plays in particular—it's infinitely more baroque, more mad—as if, as a result of reading and rereading the author's texts, you have ended up penetrating the secret of his very dreams, perhaps those of his entire century.

M. B.: In writing this text I wanted to accentuate the baroque, even fantastic character of the poetics of Molière, that is, something which at its highest point belongs to him, but which most often is found obscured by the criticism and stagings. In truth it was inspired by—you see how things are complicated!—a very beautiful text of Victor Hugo entitled "Promontorium Somnii" (*The Promontory of the Dream*), which was intended to be the preface to his "William Shakespeare," but which was abandoned later. Hugo tells that he was walking down the Avenue of the Observatory, where he encountered Arago, who invited Hugo to follow him, had him climb up in the Observatory, led him to the astronomical telescope and asked him to put his eye to it and look carefully. Then we are privileged to a superb description of the Moon, of a sunrise on the Moon, and Arago says to him, "See! That is the Sea of Serenities. . . . That is the Promontory of Dreams!" and this last expression starts Hugo off on a long meditation on the role which dreams can play in life and literature and, at a certain moment, he comes to Molière. He describes Molière obsessed by his dreams, and one sees the well-known world of Molière all marked by hallucination. . . . This text was a discovery for me. It caused me to reread Molière in a completely different way, and that *Distant Comedy* which you mentioned is an echo, no doubt, of Hugo's passage. . . . There are all sorts of things in it which come from Molière himself: the names of the characters, the original situations, and especially the vocabulary, the language which is so characteristic of him, but it's all pulled in other directions. Each fragment is a little prose poem, mischievous, perhaps as Max Jacob would have amused himself writing. . . . I mean that the text takes Molière in his seventeenth century but, by all sorts of devices, draws him up to us.

Ch. J.: Couldn't one say that starting with a well-known classic author you succeed that way in producing what Francis Ponge himself was able to produce starting with ordinary objects, which he called "object-games"? Let's think of "Soap." You remember it probably. . . . The book consists of notes dated from day to day and year to year, which are repeated, corrected, filled out very slowly. And then, suddenly, one discovers that the poem is written, and that it doesn't appear as a description of the object but rather as a sort of soap itself, although it's made of words. . . . It's the sort of little text you need only read and reread each time you feel like washing your mouth and mind completely out, just as you need only use soap to wash your hands. . . . The text of Ponge is a eulogy of soap as well as a soap usable just with a quick glance. Couldn't one say that, in the same way, your texts on Molière or Perrault, or those more ambitious ones on such and such an entire country or continent (the trajectory of *Boomerang* covers the whole territory of the Earth and almost all its history), that these texts therefore constitute at once eulogies, descriptions, and also veritable concretizations of the (work of) the author or the country which is its subject?

M. B.: Indeed, it's a little like that. You see, in texts of this kind, the juxtaposition of diverse elements can be produced within the same sentence, or even, sometimes, within the same word. The sentence will change color, tone, will change eras in passing—and that implies, of course, to be appreciated, a certain literary culture. . . . That creates a literary object endowed with very subtle and very specific properties, a sort of talisman which will permit the reader to travel very quickly in space and in time. . . . Yes, I think that's really what you feel. . . . Within these little texts one travels as if inside little rockets!

IV. OFF-CENTERING

Ch. J.: Up to now we've talked a lot about divisions, limits, frontiers and the impossibility we face today of being satisfied with them. . . . I'd now like to talk about the center. During one of our preceding conversations you said, "There is no longer a center!" Such an assertion deserves some commentary! Let me approach the subject from the most directly biographical point of view. You were born at Mons-en-Beroeul, in the north, but from the age of three spent your whole childhood and youth in Paris. In this capital you enjoyed a certain notoriety very early; you associated with the whole fashionable society of the Republic of Letters; you were admitted into the narrow circle of "great intellectuals" of the time (the ones whose names make all young provincials like me dream)—and then one day you left all that to settle finally in Nice, where you've been living now for about fifteen years and where we find you again today. Why? No, don't reply immediately. I want to state my question precisely. You took up a teaching career. I know that you taught at Sens, then in Egypt, then a little all over the world and now you are a professor at Geneva. . . . I also know your taste for travel; we've had occasion to bring it up often. . . . But that isn't what my question addresses: these risks, these follies, these necessities of life! You could have come back to Paris, but you didn't. You keep yourself far from the center, aside, withdrawn, in a retreat which does not resemble retirement at all, only at a distance. . . . In settling here, you have displaced the center of gravity of your life, and I would like to know what this decision corresponds to?

M. B.: I have to tell you I feel the cold terribly.

Ch. J.: Come, come, dear Michel Butor! You're giving me an answer like Glenn Gould! You're joking!

M. B.: No, no, it's very serious! I have the feeling of having been cold throughout my entire childhood—which can only be an illusion. But it's true that I was very cold through all the years of the Occupation, which I spent in Paris, and that I was also hungry. And the first time I lived outside France happened to be in Egypt and for me that was an extraordinary discovery—that one could live without being cold, that one could feel comfortable. . . . Because in Egypt it's dry and hot during most of the year. . . . I felt very good, I liked that very much, and it was from that moment on that I dreamed of living in a country in the south. . . . I must add also that I taught next at the University of Manchester, which was much more advantageous on the professional level.

Ch. J.: Wasn't it there that you wrote *Time Schedule,* where you describe the guilty city of Bleston for us?

M. B.: Just so. . . . Thus a city much more advantageous for me on the professional level, but where I shivered and was very unhappy. . . . Then there was Salonica, which was not so warm as Egypt but just the same much better than Manchester, and finally the Far West! Well, there I was very happy. . . . There was sunshine and it was really very dry! In the daytime it was warm and the nights were cool! And then, after a year in New Mexico, I had an invitation to teach at the University of Nice. I thought the climate might suit me here, and I wasn't mistaken, which explains why I stayed here.

Ch. J.: That was in 1970!

M. B.: Yes, in '70. . . . But I don't want to give you the idea I'm avoiding your question or that it brings nothing to mind!

Ch. J.: I. . . .

M. B.: No, it's true that I liked the Parisian literary life very much the way I was able to live it, particularly in the fifties. . . . When André Breton came back from the United States it is true that the wildest hopes were given voice. Then, there was the influence of Sartre, very important, and then everything that came afterward: the New Novel, the New Criticism. . . . All that was very exciting and I had the good luck to participate in it very closely. . . . But already the war had marked the end of something, a decline that was to be felt more and more clearly later on. You see, between the two wars Paris had been the world capital of painting and, probably, of literature, too. But with the war things were transformed. Many things happened in the United States during the war and right afterward—and that's something the French, especially those in Paris, had a very hard time admitting!

I came to realize it by traveling. Each time I returned to Paris I was surprised to note a certain narrow-mindedness. Parisians were less and less in touch with what was going on elsewhere, less and less curious. From time to time they had to try all the same to make up for lost time. They woke up; but that never lasted very long and was done only with infinite reticence, rather against their will. Then I realized that I saw (judged) things much better when I was far from Paris. I was teaching at Sens as you recalled, but because it wasn't far away I was able to live with my parents in Paris. I went to Sens to give my courses, but continued to spend all my weekends at St. Germain-des-Prés. When I left Paris it was because of problems which I already had with the French university establishment. After my third failure at the state teaching examination in philosophy I said to myself, "This can't go on this way indefinitely."

Ch. J.: It was a repeated failure at the same examination which gave us, I think, Michel Tournier's conversion to the novel also.

M. B.: Yes, Michel Tournier was one of my friends. We failed together. . . . I couldn't continue that way. I had personal problems and very serious intellectual problems. There was something that didn't work for me in what was happening in the literary world, and especially there were things which didn't work in what I was doing myself. I absolutely had to get away, and for that Egypt appeared to suit me perfectly. First, because it was far and the weather was good. . . . It was far, not only on the map, in distance, but also as a civilisation and from a linguistic point of view. . . . And then there was its mythic character which was very important. . . . For me, Egypt was first of all that of the Pharoahs, thus that of a very prestigious and very distant antiquity. And then it was Thebaïd, I mean the classic place of meditation, of retreat. . . . I needed a retreat, and that one was very profitable to me. On coming back to Paris I was delighted to be in Paris again, of course, but already I saw things from a different perspective. I no longer functioned as before, and I no longer functioned like a certain number of my friends. Then I understood that these journeys were altogether necessary to me and I sought to take more and more, to be able to have a kind of triangulation, if you understand me, in regard to Parisian ideas.

For many of my friends and comrades I was, and still am, a traitor to the Parisian Cause. I'm someone who, well! I wasn't born in Paris, but I was nourished in Paris, and I have to say that as soon as I entered the literary life and that of the art galleries, well, I was a spoiled child. I have had all sorts of problems in my career, with the university as well as with editors, but nevertheless I was a spoiled child in Paris. That is something which I can't forget; nourished by the seraglio, I left the seraglio and now am no longer part of it. Yes, it's true, I have a very strong feeling of no longer being a part of Parisian literary life, especially since I've settled in

Nice. First, for awhile I lived at Sainte-Geneviève-des-Bois in the southern suburbs, about 9 miles from Orly Airport, and already the narrow-mindedness of some Parisians was such in the sixties that I had the feeling of having crossed the Rubicon. My friends seemed to have as much trouble coming to visit me as if I had lived in Samarkand! But just the same, nothing was truly lost yet. I could go to Paris very often; I could even make long stays in foreign countries. . . . For example, I spent the whole year of 1964 (and even a little more) in West Berlin, but I felt like a delegate from the Parisian world. It was as if I were on a mission, but I had not yet changed the center of gravity of my life. . . . It's when I settled in Nice! Then I knew I was no longer part of the Parisian literary life; and since then, each time I return to Paris I find many things which interest me, of course, but ultimately I feel like a foreigner there. I'm received with much kindness, like a kind of international mini-star, but I'm no longer a Parisian coming home. I no longer feel at home there.

Obviously, I could move back to Paris, take up my place again in that literary life, but that would require a huge exertion, and it would take a long time. I would have to spare no effort, and now I no longer want to, since I find it's just not worth the trouble. The Paris I knew around the time of the war no longer exists. It was a city where life was pleasant and relaxed, but things deteriorated, especially during the sixties and seventies, and now Paris is no longer the city of my childhood. . . . Some shreds remain, of course, but it's a city which has been profoundly spoiled. There are traffic and stress problems, and then there's all that very disorganized and rarely successful construction. Among everything that has been built since the war, there are very few things one would want to show, very few that can hold up against some accomplishments of some foreign countries. . . . And then, especially, the city no longer plays the role it did play—and that is something it has not yet understood, which results in its not having adapted. What Paris was in the nineteenth century and during the first half of this century was very good. . . . But Paris isn't that any more, and all the businessmen in the world know it very well!

Ch. J.: You're speaking of the intellectual center. . . .

M. B.: Perhaps the intellectual world no longer has a single center today; perhaps that unique major center exists no more! And that's something new and enthralling. It's a new state of things which offers all sorts of possibilities! I think the fact of no longer being the center isn't so serious as Parisians imagine! They do admirable things in Amsterdam, Florence, and they even do things very well in Geneva. . . . It's not necessary to be in the center to do enthralling things. But Paris had not yet succeeded in getting rid of this nostalgia for being in first place, and many projects and creations which still appear can be explained only as a function of this dream—for being the capital of the world and that of the arts in particular.

Do you remember when they opened the Pompidou Center? Some people said it was very beautiful, but well, it was perhaps a little big, it would have been interesting perhaps to make things smaller, to make several, to spread them out. . . . And what did the Director of the Center reply? "Yes, it is big when one thinks that it is the museum of Paris, but it is not big at all when one thinks of the role this museum must play for the entire world!" That's how a magnificent opportunity to show finesse and originality was missed, and that's how all sorts of rancor were given free rein.

Ch. J.: Yes. . . . Listening to you, I'm astonished to think how little the "great intellectuals" of whom France, rightly, is so proud, have been able to bend the cultural policy of their country. They haven't hesitated to become involved in political combat, but the causes they defended turned out to be very far from the arena of their own experience. They attended to the conditions of workers and prisoners, they denounced torture in Algeria, the gulag in Russia and napalm in Vietnam. . . . All that is to their credit, no doubt, but there is no cultural life without institutions and it is remarkable that none of those intellectuals was much interested in them.

M. B.: Just the same, there was Malraux! André Malraux was an important author and he became the minister and personal friend of General de Gaulle! His efforts were not at all negligible, nor his accomplishments. . . . But it is true that he remained a prisoner of the Gaullist point of view, that is to say, of the mythology of the grandeur of France.

Ch. J.: And of centralization.

M. B.: Probably. . . . Because the two things are linked! It's in fact undeniable that it's thanks to the strong centralization of France that Paris was able to become in the eighteenth and ninetenth centuries perhaps the most important city in the world. Economically, it was fairly quickly surpassed by London, but it's true that it remained the principal cultural capital until around the Second World War. And someone like Malraux was completely taken in by this mythology. But what's remarkable is that the opposition was not much more lucid. Think of Sartre! He fought. He certainly felt that there were things that didn't work very well, and he continued to fight until his death; but his political thought always remained what it was, determined by the period between two wars. One can say that the political thought of Sartre is a relic of the thought of the Popular Front. That was when his perception of things was designed. And questions of planetary off-centering and of off-centering of all reality, well! it was something he didn't feel at all. These are things, you see, that we're only beginning to feel. I was sensitized to it fairly early because I had the good fortune to be, at a time when I was still fairly young, when I was still sufficiently malleable, in places where this off-centering was in progress. . . . I have the greatest admiration for Sartre. For thirty years he played a very important and in many respects beneficial role—in spite of a certain number of shifts, a certain number of deficiencies, a certain number of blind spells, which obligated him sometimes to change his position, which transformed his audience. . . . But you were pointing it out: all the intellectuals since the end of the war had, fundamentally, fairly little influence. They appeared to be exciting: they created works of genius sometimes, and probably these works took effect, but entirely differently from what they claimed. They wanted to be men of action, and as men of action they failed. But perhaps they weren't capable of taking a detached enough attitude. Perhaps if they hadn't sought immediate political activity, they would have felt the vastness of the problems better. With more detachment, they would have been able to appear more efficacious.

Ch. J.: Now I'd like for us to call to mind an aspect of your work as an author which will illustrate well, I think, the care you take to displace the center and to pluralize it: I mean your publishing strategy. It seems to me, indeed, that the "normal desire" of an author is to see all his books appear with the same publisher so that, finally, they will constitute a work with contours, with precise limits, easy for the reader and for criticism to find. For some years now we have seen you publish increasingly numerous and increasingly important texts with small publishers, French and foreign, to the point that it becomes, even for your most faithful readers, almost impossible to follow you. However vigilant the amateur or even the professional may be, there is always a collection of poems or a new essay to surprise him, I mean, to appear without his being able to know about it, with a publisher he didn't know existed. Your work far exceeds on all sides our ability to read it. (Don't most of your colleagues prefer to limit themselves to a new book every two or three years?) We already have to call on academics to try to keep track.

M. B.: Yes. You know, Hugo asked that they publish everything, everything they could find, and give this collection the title of *Ocean*—which seems to me very beautiful. . . . And it's true that I publish many things in different places. These are pre-publications, drafts, trial studies, in a way, because I'm linked to Gallimard. When I have a fairly voluminous, fairly important book, I am obliged to entrust it to this publisher—and I must say that things work well. These people look after me properly. But there are many things which this publishing house does not and can't do: the little *de luxe* works, works illustrated with engravings or lithographs, for example. Thus, they see no problem in my publishing them elsewhere. It very often happens that I return to these texts published here and there, rework them, cut them up in a different manner and reassemble them in a much larger volume, which I then entrust to Gallimard.

But I spoke of *de luxe*. . . . I need to clarify that there's a "poor *de luxe*" which can suit just as well as a "rich *de luxe*." I mean that these books do not need to be expensive. It does happen that I do extremely expensive books, with painters for example, but it also happens that I make little photocopied things, even some which remain in manuscript form with friends. . . . And then I can publish on the outside everything which is not mine alone: dialogues, conversations like the one we are working on here. In the long run, all these small publishers make it possible for me to publish rapidly, often in a very delicate and very pretty way, things which I can test this way.

Ch. J.: Try it out, experiment. . . .

M. B.: That's right. And I'm not the only one to do so. . . . You know that many poets proceed this way. . . . Ponge and Michaux always did. I'm always very pleased that the directors of these small publishing houses, these often venturesome firms, come to me. I'm very pleased and very flattered to be able to help them, to the extent of my means. It's certain that someone like Henri Michaux greatly helped *Fata Morgana* to become established, and that results in the French publishing fabric's being decentralized little by little. . . . Doing that, I participate in this decentralization. I am fighting—if you will, if the word isn't too strong—against the monopoly which has been able to establish itself, and I encourage people who are often young and daring. . . .

Ch. J.:   And at the same time you help a number of young authors. . . . Because it is a fact that the big Parisian publishers are no longer able to provide any training ground—not even in the journals they underwrite—for young talents. They want books that are manifestly, very obviously, successes, which results in encouraging the worst conformity. They prefer a book with very clear form, even if nothing very new happens in it, to another whose form may seem blurred, even if something new is revealed there. Now, you have certainly told us that even for an author as assured of his means as you, there is no renewal possible without experimentation, which means, without risks. And all this experimental work is nowadays taken over by the small publishers. It's absolutely necessary that they survive, that they prosper, in order that new voices not be stifled!

M. B.:   Fortunately, this fabric of small publishing houses and small journals has always existed! It already existed before the war (you remember those *Cahiers du Sud* which played such an important role!), and since the war, it has greatly developed. These small journals and houses are often ephemeral, but that isn't important! It's very annoying for those in charge of them, of course, but others replace them! What's important is that this fabric exist, that the great Parisian machines don't end up being the only ones. . . . Because, in a big house, the overhead is very high, and as a result they are obliged to earn a lot of money very quickly. When there are 150 people to pay each month, small printings are impossible; they have to have books that sell quickly. Whereas for the small craftsman, the enthusiast, sales can remain very modest. If a book is moving well, so much the better! One can think about doing another one. If not, the loss won't have been overwhelming and one just needs to wait awhile to recover one's fortunes.

Ch. J: We should also talk about all the new processes: offset, photocopy, which perhaps allow one to dream of a kind of widespread self-publication.

M. B.:   No doubt! This dream has become less fanciful than it was a few years ago. With the word processors and photocopiers that we have available now, it's become possible for anyone at all to make known what he writes. Young writers can set up a publishing cooperative. They can print the number of copies that seems suitable to them; then, they'll need to undertake a little finishing off and handling. That's entirely within the reach of a small number of individuals in their leisure time, and that permits things to be circulated, and that, a few years ago, was very difficult.

Ch. J.: And criticism will still have to cooperate! It's in the center, you know. It holds the center and is insistent that this center not go displacing itself, or pluralizing itself, or relativizing itself! I don't doubt that this movement of off-centering has become irresistible. But those who are in charge of thinking often have great difficulty in even seeing what's already being done.

M. B.: Habits will have to change, and it's true that these are very longstanding, and it will take time. . . . But aren't we already at work?

V. PLACE

Ch. J.: Don't you think that what distinguishes most clearly a fictional or poetic work from philosophy is the question of place? We love the words, the very varied forms of the sentences, but we never manage to forget the scene. The scene involves us, informs us, and informs our sentences. When we speak or write, it's a question of place as well as of us. . . . It had to be therefore, dear Michel Butor, that the place you have chosen to live should suit the writer. . . .

M. B.: A long time ago they asked me to answer that famous questionnnaire called "Proust's," and I remember that to the question, "Where would you like to live?" I answered, "In a big city on the seashore." There are many cities located on the seashore, of course, but most often the sea isn't visible from the cities themselves. Think of Marseilles! While here, the relief is such that the sea is visible everywhere, present everywhere. And then, Nice is the meeting of opposites: there's the sea. . . .

Ch. J.: And the mountain looking down on us. . . .

M. B.: Which we cling to. . . . From my window, I can see the sea and the peaks. . . . I'm in the middle of gardens planted with mimosas and palms and, opening my window in winter I can see peaks covered with snow! It's something I have probably looked for all my life, a sort of miracle which occurs sometimes, in certain regions of the world, like Greece, Japan, or California. . . . It's also a symbol, because, in almost all cases, there is someone saying to you, "You really have to choose! You cannot have both this *and* that. You really must give up one *or* the other." And no, indeed, I do not like to give up. There are thus those places where Nature demonstrates to us the falseness of the old aphorism: regions differing from reality are not necessarily exclusive, and opposites can meet. . . . Here, because of the dryness of the air, the mountain is very visible. On the northwest coast of the United States or Canada, you also have this meeting of mountain and ocean, but it all goes on in the clouds, with occasional breakthroughs, sudden openings, which are very moving. . . .

Ch. J.: One of your early books (it was *Interlude,* I think) was already dedicated "to the frontiersmen"!

M. B.: We are here on the frontier! It's true that I like crossing frontiers; frontiers irritate me and I have to cross them! Each time it's like transgressing a taboo. . . . We've talked about the frontier in the history of the United States. Here, it would only be a frontier between two nations. Living near a frontier cannot be like living in the heart of the country. There are people in Nice for whom Italy is only Vintimiglia, where two or three times a year they go to buy handbags or shoes. That's not much, to be sure! But it's the beginning of an opening. And then, there's this very important fact, that Nice hasn't been French for a very long time, that it hasn't always been a part of the famous hexagon! In its own history, Nice has crossed a frontier. It's a transient city, a city which has passed from one sphere of influence to the other. . . . In the same way, if I like Geneva a lot—and you know I go almost every week from Nice to Geneva and from Geneva to Nice—it's because it's also a frontier city. When you're in Geneva and the weather's clear, you know that all the mountains you see surrounding the city and forming the horizon are French. Your feet are here and your gaze is elsewhere, in another country! Without mentioning all the international institutions which cause all languages to be spoken there.

Ch. J.: And there is, as at that most beautiful moment in American history, immediate proximity of the immense reserves which mountains and sea constitute. Population reserves or wilderness stocked here and now with plants and animals which are silent witnesses of the mists of our time!

M. B.: There are those boats! . . . I remember, two years ago, I was on the northwest coast of Canada, on the island of Vancouver and, one day, with a friend, we left to take a trip farther north. We crossed the whole length of the island, that is, we covered more than 300 miles to take a boat which was to carry us to the Alaskan frontier. While passing thus between the American continent and the island coasts, following what they call the "Inner Passage," we met a splendid ship. It was night, the ship was white and all lit up, and it slipped along without making any noise on that very black water and, as it went by, we were able to read its name: it was called the *Golden Odyssey,* and we remembered it. . . . Well! A few weeks later when I was back in Nice strolling along the port with my dog Jonas, what did I see? The *Golden Odyssey* at the dock among the others. . . . That was the one! Thus, there are these ships, from all the corners of the world with such evocative names! . . . Then, you are right about mountains. You pass very abruptly from one climate to the next. You need only follow the canyon, I mean the valley of the Roya or of the Vesubie. You change vegetation and climate completely, and you change habits. In a very few miles you travel a great deal, and that is why I like this region so much!

Ch. J.: As for the city itself, unfortunately, it has hardly been spared more than Paris.

M. B.: People who have lived here a long time, especially since the war, probably have many reasons to complain! But as for me, I arrived when the disease was already well advanced! It seems to me that the main attraction of the city was its gardens. The grand hotels of the beginning of the century were all surrounded by magnificently planted parks. Nice is probably one of the places in the world where they have been able to acclimatize the largest number of foreign species.

Ch. J.: The art of gardens is moreover that of moving frontiers?

M. B.: I have under my window specimens from the entire world! Great torch-thistles which remind me of Arizona but which must come from Peru. . . . Daturas which must come from the Canaries. . . . Australian mimosas and eucalyptus. . . . And if one has traveled a little and has a little interest in botany, all these plants are like windows open on the "Inner Passage." But now many of the gardens have been destroyed. The city has spread out. As you turn a corner, you may find yourself in a suburban California decor, completely loony, but not without charm. . . .

Ch. J.: We always come back to this American dream! In everything that you say, Nice appears to be the most American city of our old Europe. I really like the image of a "loony California suburb. . . ." I see in it certain streets of Saint-Laurant-du-Var, of Cagnes, or of Juan-les-Pins. We probably still lack the *Big Sur* of Henry Miller; I mean, some of those little communities of artists and intellectuals all busy with soft energy, repetitive music and spirituality. . . . And then we've been much taken up with beaches, wind-surfing and tourism, but we don't seem to believe very much that one day our *Sophia Antipolis* could be compared to Silicon Valley.

M. B.: I like this American aspect very much, but I also like the very varied Edwardian architecture very much! These palaces surrounded by gardens, these whimsical billionaires' villas, some of which remain but others which we must fear will be soon be destroyed, like the rest! You know the beautiful book by Cuchi White? Well, you should know that a good number of the buildings photographed in it have been destroyed in the course of the last two or three years! Yes, there's still in Nice a veritable museum of architecture which ought to interest all the champions of "post-modernism." We find here, side by side, not reproductions of other monuments, but veritable projections of dreams. They dreamed of a Greek villa, fourth century, in the style of Delos. They dreamed of a Russian isba, a Moorish palace, Italian-style archways, Gothic churches, and British cottages. . . . and they built them! And then, in the old city there's that group of baroque churches, much closer to those one sees in Genoa or even in Naples than anywhere else in France! And I'm not mentioning the surrounding villages which take you back to the Middle Ages. . . . or Terra Amata, with that incredible story of the shifting of the coast. . . .

Ch. J.: I asked you about our city and, right away, you talked to me of the art of gardens, that is, an art which consists in bringing species of the most different origins together. . . . And when it's a question of architecture, it's again this baroque "post-modern" heteroclicity which you emphasize. . . . As for me, I would add that if, beyond this principle of heteroclicity, the architecture of Nice has a feature which is its own, it's certainly that of painted façades, and more exactly, *trompe-l'œil* . . . For centuries, the walls of Nice have been painted in *trompe-l'œil*—like California walls again! And what that means, it seems to me, is that in Nice as in all the books of Michel Butor, the origin slips away! In this city, at its most ancient, at its mythical point of origin and authenticity, one finds only a smile and a game.

M. B.: One finds only the passage.

Third Part
EXAMPLES

I. SELF-PORTRAIT OF THE SEVENTIES

For Roger Borderie

Who are you, Michel Butor?
I am a sickness,
I am a stomach heavy as a trunk stuffed with books, I am two feet that must
      be washed often,
. I am a leaden sleep and a rusty insomnia,
  I am a burning blindness and a deafness lying in wait,
 . I am a nomad made faint by the sight of a suitcase,
I am an insatiable appetite and a slow digestion,
I am a coal miner and an expert in mine-sweeping,
I am a mud head with serpent skin,
I am a spermatozoon in all stages of its life cycle.

Where do you come from, Michel Butor?
I descend not only from the monkey but also from the snail,
I come from mud and drool,
. I come from gurgling and panting,
 . I come from soot and surliness, I come from thirst and desire, .
I come from ash-heaps and garbage dumps, I come from rubble and
      saltpeter,
I come from obstinacy and evasion, I come from heresies and deadlocks,
I come from stench and pus, I come from blood, phlegm, and groans,
. I come from a warm womb in a rainy suburb,
I come from bacteria and worms as well as from university moles,
      philosophical or not,
I come from spitballs and all the dunces,
I come from hospitals, morgues, and senility,
. I come from an explosion no one knows too much about.

Where are you, Michel Butor?
I am not only falling between two chairs but am between two soils, not only
        on the fence between two waters but between two Earths,
        not only between youth and age, but between two eras,

I am in a suburb of our time, in transit, I drag from customs office to
customs office, stagger from train station to train station,
I am hunting in the jungle of words,
I am in full drainage, in full diarrhea, in crumbling collapse,
I avoid bars and brothels, I find myself caught in their web again by surprise, I gain little from them, I inscribe them, I absorb them,
eject them, dislocalize them; distill them, crystallize them,
I am betweeen the here and the now, between the elsewhere and the hence-
forth, between the center and the yet again, between the
fringe and the fire,
I am near an airport.

Where are you going, Michel Butor?
I go toward chinks in the Iron and Bamboo Curtains, the withering of the
State,
Toward skidding and giddiness, toward fainting and lull,
Toward the unfolding horizon, the changing weather, the eye of the cy-
clone, phosphorescent quagmires, laughing ghosts, inverted
volcanos, opened Sun, opera of speeds, rejuvenating
hunger,
Toward the revolutions-gravitations sweet like a woman waking up warm-
ing herself at the blaze of outdated laws,
Toward insults, gibes, hissings, and signs of impatience,
Toward the dough-troughs for texts, the ovens for images, the fishponds
for silences,
Toward the worst disappointment, jilting, ingratitude, repudiation, contempt
and mistakes, toward the assembly of the senses for a
decision on the final plunge.

What are you doing, Michel Butor?
I am trying to sell a little house in a Parisian suburb in order to fix up farther
south a sort of modest observatory-warehouse where my
aims will be able to appease their madness—not so easy,
I rear children who scream and play scales, I look at theories turning inside
out like jackets,
I seek to reform human understanding, to find again in the pit of the present
moment something perpetually forgotten for centuries, I

scratch, I search, I scent, I unearth, I gnaw, I ruminate, I
    chew again, I begin again, I get lost in the search, I sink,
I prepare snares and traps, I sound, I aim, set out the decoys,
I scratch out, I tear up, I get entangled, I dry up, I bang my head against the
    walls, I despair, I bite my nails, tear out my hair, black my
    eyes, rely on my guts,
Rage, become unhinged, go astray, split in two, lament, find out,
In suspense.

II. BEFORE THE DIALOGUE OF THE LIVING
For Henri Maccheroni

We are between the sea and the mountain,
between salt and snow, sun and storm, sky and roofs,
Between France and Foreign, between Provence and Comté, exile and
origin, archanthropians and pensioners,
Between city and suburb, orange groves and high-rises, olives and pines,
Between airport and seaports, between train stations and footpaths,
Between customs office and frontier;

We are between envelope and letter, between print and page, words and
blank spaces, consonants and vowels,
Between spot and ring, between water color and pencil, figure and
commentary, ideogram and flow,
Between color and speech, between theme and scheme, trademark and
legend,
Between discourse and fame;

We are between hammer and anvil, between two wars and two trails, the
mass and the shedding, between vertigo and veering,
Between tree and bark, between bow and arrow, wound and knife, blows
and bruises,
Between switch and spark, between energy and matter, pucker and whistle,
Between wall and shadow, between exhalation and halo,
Between margin and reverse;

We are between eye and tears, between heart and blood, urine and shit, hair
and mucous,
Between teeth and tongue, between hunger and thirst, skin and bones, dust
and spittle,
Between claw and fingernail, between horrors and orisons, murder and
tenderness,
Between legs and orifices, between sperm and milk,
Between lip and kiss;

We are between pith and peel, between courtyard and garden, stamens and
        pistil, furs and feathers,
Between pear and cheese, between daydog and nightwolf, numeral and
        number, act and outlook,
Between pose and take, between sighs and memory, walk and step,
Between childhood and suffering, between sense and silence,
We are between life and death.

III. RAIN ON THE FRONTIERS

For Philip Hélénon

Beet fields up to the barbed wire, bordered by paths where cyclists chase each other; bushes of mistrust, with tufts of feathers torn from the chests of their fluttering victims by starving cats. Long ago there were some houses here. Fragments of walls remain with disemboweled fireplaces, even several rags of tapestry finishing their fading. Briars have invaded the living room, clematis reigns in the kitchen. Where the lawn was, a pond with birds of passage who take turns according to the seasons. Mattress springs rust on the bank. By this road one reaches the customs and police barracks, barriers and chains, lines of cars waiting in exasperation, police caps and boots, revolvers in their holsters. Clouds and waves pass by.

This way the dunes, blue thistles, some reeds around the puddles, smugglers' paths, used now only for picnics. A ray of sun between the laundry dripping on the russet countryside, awakening a fragment of windowglass fallen on a wild rose bush at the edge of the huts; a sketch of a rainbow rapidly scrubbed away by the dishcloths of winter, and then the downpour starts again with a discouraging regularity, fogging up the lenses of my glasses, while I flounder at the edge of the forbidden empty lots, hands in pockets of my no longer waterproof overcoat, whistling under my breath an old protest song.

Turning the page, here are some traces of melting snow. The dead leaves stick to my boots whose laces I will soon have to tie again. That bell tower, those trees even, are on the other side. People who avail themselves of their shelter speak another language, obey other laws, observe other rules of hygiene, take other drugs to try to cure their ills. I have never been to see; I would have to take too roundabout a way. But I shall go one day, coming from somewhere else. I shall have shown my passport very far from here. I shall come clandestinely as far as the village, under a false name perhaps, after having let my beard grow, and no one will suspect that I know the other half of this scarred region so well, the other lip of this gash, the other side of these curtains of thick fogs and thorns, the hidden face of this silence pierced by cries and combustions. I shall go some day when the weather is good.

Soaked to the skin I have walked along this barren track, these mined terraces, these clearings rutted by the caterpillar tracks of tanks, these concrete dragons' teeth flaying the old skin of the burnt woods, hiding when I saw the sentinels under their dark variegated banners lying in wait to see if they could escape their military boredom by tracking some transgressor, diluting their longing with his torture. But their distant feet soon changed direction; I knew they could no longer make me out against a background as drab as I, and I took my explorations up again, sleeping sometimes in ditches as if it were still wartime, because the sadness and the haunting memory of the war are always there, and because from one minute to the next some one of these drops of water could be transformed into a drop of lead.

Oh, rain, erase these frontiers for us, wash our continents of these stripes inflicted in honeyed tones by the diplomatic whip of amiable madmen during interminable discussions in pavilions with pendants and marquetry; carry us away in your immense babble, in your tranquil canter toward those other frontiers which do not correspond to any line traced on a map, guarded by no army, marked by no placards, in those regions where the contours of knowledge rush down in cataracts, into abysses which make them blaze up. Frontiers, give us your rain! Oh, rains of the frontiers, wash away our partitions and our wounds; sweep us away to the other side of the frontiers of the rain, lash our sluggishness and dissolve us in the delights of germinating and vaporizing, filtering with emotion through all the walls of our bodies and of the hours.

IV. BRIDGES

For Vieira da Silva

Plunging on the paths, the arsenals, the electric power stations, the stadiums, one steps over the highways, the overpopulated or forested valleys, and on the other side it is another language, another look, another way of eating, of making the bed, of rearing the children. One level for trains, another for automobiles, a passage reserved for pedestrians, with high closely woven wire netting to discourage suicides, but in any case one ends up at barriers, barbed wires, suspicions, sluggishness, and the morgue. The great arches invite one to flight, and then the brutal fall back down. One has the impression of being beaten black and blue. Do we really need to go away? Anything rather than remain in place wallowing in one's own stews. To save his son, Dedalus, locked up in his own labyrinth, trying vainly to reconstruct its lost and betrayed plans, made jointed wings for him, covered with swan feathers, some say eagle or even crow. The apprenticeship was long and difficult; they tried the most ancient footbridges; the tight-wire artists, trapeze acrobats, lent their nets, their gear, their straps. But when finally they could leave all the leading-strings behind, what a joy for a few hours to skim over the cupolas, minarets, and spires, to carry bouquets to deliciously stupefied girls on the fortress battlements they were visiting escorted by their terrified professors! And he accompanied helicopters, amused himself following at full speed the planes taking off, to the applause of choirs of celestial messengers with the accompaniment of the passionate percussion of the 49 tribes of demons, who had finally succeeded, thanks to him, in having their claims heard in the office of the upper administration in a state of grave unrest; a few hours, his great flight lasted only a few hours; when he appeared above the traffic, there was bewilderment everywhere. They took him for the young destroyer announced by the scriptures in which very few, in the last analysis, in spite of all their bragging, did not still believe, and certain sects started up fires on both banks. However, he was so beautiful: waltzes of shoulders and wing-quills, braids of phalanges and slipstreams; it couldn't be helped. Barrages were fired, with retorts, traffic jams on all the roads. The outflanked platoon chiefs had their red alerts sounded and the explosive charges provided in advance in the reactors, to the snickering from hypocrites, badly hidden by their oily tears—because, rubbing their eyes, they could not help rubbing their hands together also—did their job noisily: detonation, deflagration, conflagration. So many victims! Nothing remained any more but ruins like twisted arms lamenting here and there, similar to ancient war machines on the horizons of Carthage, and the funeral services with embarrassed speeches by military and civilian authorities. The most thoughtful neighborhoods add an epilogue to the legend, claiming that his body became entirely a murmur in the air and that people hear him encouraging us when we cross the reconstructed bridge, more solid and more massive, with increased safety measures. However, in spite of the touching columns raised up here and there by the tottering governments, most of the time we can believe that he did nothing, and no one for the moment is planning to renew his attempt, because what we are all waiting for, which will be the true monument to his memory, illuminated by suggestions from his passes, is another bridge going from heart to heart of our countries, is that all our countries, our cities, become bridges.

V. POST NO BILLS

For Janine

Behind this wall grind the pumps of unhappiness which the police-men fill with toothaches! Do not come near! The staff officer shakes his decorations on the rusty footbridges, sprinkling oil on the mossy crank-arms, and the bailiffs wipe their sharplinked chains with scraps of skin which they fold up again in their pockets like handkerchiefs. Look for the way out! The generals cackle behind the grills of their masks and vomit in their caps while rocking on cast-iron swings attached to the bells tolling the knell. Are you alone? The administration dozes in its bloodied featherbeds, its swimming pools of phlegm, its salons panelled with abcesses and ulcers. Be sure they are not spying on you! The secretaries gnaw their nails, the treasurers delouse their favorite pigs, who shudder with disgust. Huddled in their overheated dens, the chaplains rub their hands together, the ambas-sadors lose their dentures in the champagne glasses while the squall of hiccups passes from receptions to private viewings. Prick up your ears! They show each other their collections of slums, while preparing without weakness their next match of wargames, strike-breaking, or standardiza-tion. Redouble your caution! One-eyed bell-hops pass out cigars before the emery-cloth curtains are opened on the one-armed ballerinas. Look behind you! The gardeners rake their rubble lawns with a bulldozer, the hostesses arrange bouquets of faded brooms in the voting boxes in front of marzipan statues of the preceding municipal councilors, which their successors nibble at distractedly during the course of the next meeting of the pollution com-mission. Not a sound! They admire the plans of shopping malls under construction with their immense windowless corridors, their sumptuous water-leaked frescos, their vacant lots cunningly filled with potholes, their parapets surreptitiously chipped. Watch out! The accident officials are designing new entrances to highways, the catastrophe specialists are study-ing interesting sites for airports and fascinating projects for dams. They are watching you. In their laboratories papered with broken glass, doctors in gold lamé rags sort out the most dangerous mutations, and laureate authors in their colleges with corrugated cardboard cupolas prepare their best-sellers. Come back tonight! In the great pheasant hatcheries they accelerate the greening of the carrion; in the ultra-modern polluteries they whitewash in assembly lines. Danger is threatening you. In the suffocateries they test gags, in the voodooeries they tape speeches, in the gasperies they wear out the rebels, in the benumberies they select from childhood those who will know how to collaborate in this great work of misery. Time is not ripe. Gently, they put out their eyes on the day of their initiation while filling their mouths with milk caramel and marshmallow.

Behind this wall stretches another city entirely built on granite pilings above a phosphorescent sea. Wait for a chance! By day light comes from above, by night from down below. The police arrive. In the twilight there is a moment when on the outside all shadows disappear; objects are lit up by two lights of different colors but equal intensity. Watch out. Men are markedly smaller here; one who reaches the height of three feet would be considered a giant. They are setting a trap for you. On the other hand, certain animal species benefit by considerable growth: their tomtits are as big as swans, their swans are used as horses. Walk on tiptoe! The stables are on the roofs. In the greatest silence! Open carriages have built-in airbags; they can skim over the water flashing forth sprays of glimmerings. Search the blind alleys! This wall is guarded on their side by police as severe as ours. Shadows move. The official point of view, repeated on innumerable pennants dragged along by black swans, is that the wall does not exist, that the world stops here. The sewers are stuffed with earphones. Behind this wall—which does exist, says our official point of view without ever speaking of it—we don't know what there is and we are forbidden to ask the question. Take care! The policemen in their perpetual rounds never look at it. Don't say anything! They are there to keep anyone at all from approaching. Don't make a move! These policemen, besides, although feared and respected, are not considered men; they are castrated and their voices are in great demand for the choirs. Turn around! Putting your ear to the partition, perhaps you will hear scraps of their concerts accompanied on the lute with profound virtuosity in antique modes of polished quaintness. Not another step! An insistant rumble murmurs that these are the guardians of the seraglio world, these are the volunteers tempted by the inreased height and brute force which their mutilation procures for them and the metallic hue which little by little cloaks their skin. Patience! They succeed in persuading themselves that they have become machines; all the vocabulary which concerns them is marked by it. Hide! One does not say of a policeman that he eats, but that he fills his tank, not that he urinates, but that he drains. Put on a mask! He does not speak, but squeaks. Conceal yourself! He does not have arms, but levers, not ears but receivers, not eyes but lamps, not nostrils but sensors, not feet but propulsors. Flee! He does not rest, he is put away, not in a house, but in a shed. Don't come near! His bed is his crate, his chairs are his props, and his clothing, his wrapping. Look for the way out! The climate is of an unequaled mildness, and if the houses have walls it is for fighting off light, not cold. Are you alone? Extremely modest, they do not touch one another, *a fortiori* do not kiss, and especially do not embrace except behind closed doors; but on our side of the wall, in spite of policemen's rounds, their houses have no partitions because the wall blocks a good part of the light. Be sure they are not spying on you! Sneaking a peek through a crack you will perhaps succeed in seeing some of their revels, which do not interest the policemen at all. Prick up your ears! In their dreams they picture us, they admire us, they envy and pity us at the same time. Redouble your caution! They would like us to take them in our arms. Look behind you! They count secretly on our assistance without which, without one of our glances, so the superstitions say, they cannot adequately make love.

VI. IN THE MEANTIME

For Pierre Canou

In the meantime the beard has grown
the hair has turned white
the wrinkles have multiplied
the gaze is a little farther lost in the distance

Old friends have disappeared
young affections have been born
enemies have wearied
new ones have broken out

A few hundred scribbled pages
have come to rejoin their elder sisters
in the sub-basements of the municipal library
and the books on the shelves have gained a few decimeters

The currencies have continued their fluctuations
the Sun climbing the degrees of the zodiac
the arsenals on all borders have perfected their missiles
whose targets the incessant war has displaced

In spite of all efforts the frantic race has continued
while memories modified their lighting
the dust frosting the windows of childhoods
and the future has changed color like a maple leaf in autumn.

VII. BETWEEN THE DROPS

For Vincent Bioulès

My dear Vincent,

What a pleasure for me to welcome you to Nice, to this city to which I have become so attached, but what a problem, since the short time we have prevents my seeing the works you are going to show! I am in my Genevan bedroom and I have to wait to be again in my house at the Antipodes to be able to immerse myself at least a little in the contemplation of some of your early or recent works in order to respond to the request you have just made me by phone. I hope to get it written for you this weekend. It is Wednesday; I am leaving to give my seminar on the *Fifth Book* of Rabelais.

*

* *

I am in the plane. I think of you and of this text which I must write for you. I leaf through my appointment book and panic begins to overwhelm me. How am I going to manage to slip the creation of these few pages in among all that is already planned, already promised? It would be best if I could get it typed up for you on Pentecost Sunday. No mail on Monday. The letter thus will not be able to get off until Tuesday; with a little luck you will have it Wednesday, more likely Thursday. We are descending toward the sea, and that reminds me of all that is Mediterranean in what you do. Your coming to Nice is Languedoc stepping over Provence to come caress Italy. But they are asking us to put up the tray tables of our seats.

*

* *

I am in my office at the Antipodes. When I arrived, I got a piece of bad news from my travel agent: impossible to get a seat for Geneva Monday during the day. The only way is to leave this very day. The schedule I had planned for myself flies to pieces. Very far from being able to describe some of your works at leisure, I must content myself with very hastily reassembling some brief impressions, leafing through them, casting a glance in order to have somewhat fresher memories.

*

* *

I am on the plane between Nice and Geneva. It is Pentecost, a day which makes me think of Saint Mark in Venice and in particular of that cupola of the baptistry where one sees the twelve apostles dispersing themselves in all the directions of the Earth of that time, each with his flame on his head. Metal birds now take us across rivers, oceans, and mountains. Wires and waves transmit sparks of information for us, and I wonder if upon my arrival I am not going to find an anxious message from you. But no, not yet; forgive me. Thus I think of you while looking at peaks and valleys, glaciers and villages. On some roofs there are solar discs. It is your painting of yesteryear, those rectangles of pigment which absorb light in order to restore it to us in energy, warmth, sweetness, with those layers which one sees passing one over the other in such a way that one has the impression that the day's fingers are slipped behind the first surfaces to ripen in the depths, to imbue even the fibers and to diffuse themselves on the whole wall, on all the house around; and it is your painting of today whose representation only explains better and better what is happening between layers whose sensitivities respective to excitement, as in the switch of a thermostat, provoke twistings, contrastings, recessings, warnings. Here is the Turquoise of the lake already. I have to stuff this draft in my bag before passing through customs.

*
* *

I am in my office at the Faculty of Letters in Geneva. I have just heard a thesis defense on the colors of Elstir and, before becoming absorbed in rereading the last dramatic works of Claudel or, to put it better, of his last booklets with theater in mind, to prepare my upcoming course on this author and the Far East, I glance at the first formless notes I sketched out on paper already a week ago toward this preface that I promised you, that I promised myself to write for you, and which is getting later and later. The problem is, I do not have my typewriter with me, and, as I have to spend next weekend in Paris, I will not rejoin that old companion or accomplice again until much too late, and I will only be able to send a hand-written text to you in that house in Montpellier which comes back to me in memory, house of memory, observatory from which you study the moods and wanderings of the child you were, his explorations in the school garden up to that grating which is now that of your garden. Did you then gaze at the windows of your studio, your office, your living room, suspecting that one day you would be there, on the other side, that you would work there, would lie in wait there, would cast ropes of color and music from there to lasso the distracted, troubled, dreamy, wondering child that you were, waiting for the whistle, the fathers' bell to summon you back to study? And now one of my students is knocking at my door.

*
* *

I am in the High-Speed Train between Geneva and Paris; I look at countryside filing past the window, which brings me back to yours, those of your paintings, prints or those of your life, of your house, with their double panes looking out over the double garden, the landscape with double background, the between-two-colors and the between-two-ages, the between-two-seasons, which leads me to take down from the rack my little black suitcase to look in it for the few notes scrawled hastily last Sunday on the subject of that set of four silk screen prints devoted to the four seasons of your house and of your windows: spring, ochre walls, open windows, flowering chestnut tree; summer, black walls, open windows, leaves of the chestnut tree, the exterior light reflected in the mirror in the middle; autumn, red walls, carafe of wine on the big table which was not there in the pre- ceding months (was it in the garden?), a celestial globe on the little table which was there, stars that one will perhaps not be able to look at outside any more and that now have to be studied indoors, windows closed, their decorations, their little panes, the night sky with its stars certainly, but like an appeal or a regret, and especially the trees completely transformed, as if the branches of the chestnuts, drooping in the previous seasons, now pruned, had kept these pines and cypresses from being seen; winter finally, mauve walls, beige furniture like this room that is perceived in the mirror, like the pines and cypresses seen through the sepia frames of the windows in front of the turquoise sky with bands of clouds like little sheep in the mountain field, or waves on the sea. And it is really today I am for the first time getting the draft of the last few days into shape; but the discomfort and the shaking of the train make my letters zigzag, scarcely legible, and thus I really will have to recopy properly all this beginning when I succeed in diverting a few minutes for it in a more stable place. At the moment the vibrations are increasing to such a point that I am going to have to give up.

*
* *

I am on the terrace of the Café Flore in Saint-Germain-des-Près. It has been many years since this has happened to me. I am waiting for two friends with whom I am to lunch. I find myself again in my adolescence, then in the days of my first publications, of our first meetings. All that has happened. All that has changed. People come out of church in vacation clothes, hurry to go vote, at least some of them. These are the elections for the European parliament. We do not even wonder who is going to win, but who is going to lose the worst. Such is the crisis. Your painting helps us to be in our time by situating us among the covers of survival and the debacle of past time, among the premonitions of the next day, the signs which stars and trees make to us, those of the boulevard, for example, which make me think of those in your gardens, your painting and your reading, because all that you do is nourished by languages and texts, and I notice, to my great shame, that I have forgotten in my rush to bring with me from Nice the lines I devoted to you formerly which could have helped me in this presentation, the *Ballad of Iris' Scarf* and its reisue in *Express,* and especially that I did not think to bring some of your classics, Baudelaire for example, whom I could have quoted here by transforming its lighting, among other things the *Former Life,* "the vast porticos" becoming the courtyards of your former school, and since I have with me, aside from some of my recent works, nothing more than the prose works of Claudel in order to prepare for my coming classes, I can detach from them this brief poem which seems to me to have been made in obscure anticipation of certain of your works as well as for those of the Japanese painter of that time, *Two Green Bamboos:*

"On a long band of paper Saïki has painted two parallel bamboos of different diameters, no leaves, nothing but the two tubes of an even green beginning with the roots. Two canes, one would say: is this a subject for a painter? But the fact that the two tubes do not have the same thickness, doesn't the eye notice that immediately, which nourishes in us the sense of proportion? Besides, don't you see that the joints which are very close together near the root then separate themselves at calculated distances which are not the same on the two stems? And from this double comparison does there not spring forth for the mind at once a harmony and a melody like the notes of a double flute? The eye does not tire of verifying that the proportion is this number which cannot be represented by any digit."

As for my manuscripts, I have with me only the next part of *Forest Sounds,* some of which I wanted to copy for another friend who cannot come until a little later; I am thus going to collect, like a faggot-gatherer, branches and twigs, some samples, in honor of your own trees:

"Like a flight of wood-pigeons my boughs, like the caresses of a river my veins. I open slowly out all my splinters in the calming of the rediscovered sun."

*
* *

"One after the other the pieces of my armor will enrich the mosses of my carpets."

*
* *

"Ants distribute their caravans along my ravines and the squirrels lay up their treasures in my armpits."

*
* *

"A green woodpecker in my buttonhole, a semi of spiders crosswise and a lizard for signature."

*
* *

I am in the 1900 restaurant in the Lyon Station. I have before my eyes these paintings which call one toward Marseilles, Toulon, Monaco, just across from me Villefranche and its harbor as it was then, scarcely inhabited. Behind Mount Boron I can spot exactly where my house at the Antipodes is located, further in the same direction, the gallery where your exhibit is going to take place, and while telling myself about the sea of these old painters whose flaming signatures no longer evoke anything in us, that I am going to have to give up writing about the role that the sea plays in your work (I will have thus to come back to it another time) and, while the glasses are clinking, that it will be the same for the music; I explain to my table companions that you have called me this very morning, worried about where I was with it, that I have therefore to conserve a certain sobriety in order to manage finally to finish the draft of this preface during my trip on the train, because the evening is to be taken up by a speech at the Museum of Art and History of Geneva, and it will take me all morning the next day to make a fair copy before going to the University, where I will have it photocopied, this text that I am in the process of finishing, and to send it to you so that it can be published on time.

VIII. ANOTHER VERSION OF *SAGA*

For Christian Jacomino

1. NARRATIVE

How to present the iceberg?
You will call it the challenge of the seals.
Now in us the madness of the pole. . . .
How to name the speaker?
You will call him the recluse of the crossroads.

2. FIRST PORT OF CALL

How to introduce the iceberg?
You will call it the challenge of the wind.
Times earlier than the sand, the sea, the sky above and the pasturelands. The Sun exists already, but one does not know where its home is. The Stars do not know their way, the Moon has no knowledge of its power. I see the gods meeting and giving names to night, morning, noon, twilight, and the divisions of the year. They come finally to a plain, where they raise up altars, temples and forges, and fashion golden tools.
How to name the reader?
You will call him the whispering of the horizons.

3. DESERT

How to tame the iceberg?
You will call it the specter of adventures.
Little by little the radiant zone rises in the sky and appears, striped with blackish bands. Rivers. Streams of a luminous substance then shoot forth, diminishing or forcing their brilliance. Black springs. The meteor, reaching its zenith, is often composed of several arcs which bathe in waves of red, yellow, or green. Cracks and straits. It is a dazzling sight. Reflections. Soon the diverse curves meet in a single point and form boreal crowns of celestial opulence. Rocks of anger. Finally the arcs press one against the other. Immobile crowds. The splendid dawn pales.

How to name the explicator?
You will call him the permanence of departure.

4. SECOND PORT OF CALL

How to venerate the iceberg?
You will call it the city of phantoms.

Leif, son of Eric the Red, sent to Norway to be baptized, came back with the mission of evangelizing Greenland, after many an adventure and many a tempest succeeded in saving some castaways who called him blessed, and, at the moment when he saw the coast of Greenland again, the hurricane drove him to a shore which he called the Country of Vines. Returning to the fjord village, he found his father again, who refused to convert, his mother, who had a church built. Digs in 1961 uncovered this building.

How to name the translator?
You will call him the vagabond of foam.

5. TRANSPARENCY

How to greet the iceberg?
You will call it the factory of abysses.
How to name the gold?
You will call it the ransom of sealskins.
How to name the sword?
You will call it bough of the wounds.
How to name the blood?
You will call it stream of the wolves.
How to name the sea?
You will call it chain of the islands.
How to name the earth?
You will call it horse of the mist.
How to name the wind?
You will call it curse of forests.
How to name silver?
You will call it ice of crucibles.

How to name the adaptor?
You will call him the diver of claws.

6. THIRD PORT OF CALL

How to glorify the iceberg?
You will call it mother of whirlpools.

     The king has me sit between two fires which burn in the middle of the room. Eight nights pass before one of his sons offers me something to drink. The fire has begun to burn my cape. I speak to the flames, make them move back, then slowly describe the dwelling of the gods, the configuration of the invisible worlds and in particular the infernal; then I reveal that they call me the Fatal, and also the Conqueror, and also the Welcome, and also the Masked. Still the king fails to identify me; I say to him then: "I see your death."
How to name the interpreter?
You will call him the survivor of forgetting.

7. MAXIMS

How to sing of the iceberg?
You will call it the guardian of shocks.

     An intense vapor rises from the snows; it is a good omen, and the melting of these immense masses seems near. The pale disk of the Sun tends to take on more color and to trace longer spirals above the horizon; night hardly lasts three hours. Another not less significant symptom, some ptarmigans, northern geese, plovers, grouse are coming back in flocks.
How to name the intermediary?
You will call him the librarian of the hard-pressed.

8. ANIMATED

How to announce the iceberg?
You will call it the reverse of midnight.

     Under the music is engulfed the end of the preceding text:
... The air is filled little by little with these deafening cries which the

navigators of last spring still remember. Hares make their appearance on the shore of the bay. . . .

How to name the messenger?

You will call him the stenographer of the crumblings.

Then begins:

And beyond Greenland we reached the Land of Fogs and Whirlwinds. . . . which will be discovered little by little in

9. ELEVATION

How to name the iceberg?

You will call it citadel of the dawn.

. . . and still farther the Land of the Shooting Stars, and still farther the Land of the Moon, and still farther the Land of the Swords, and still farther the Land of the Flashing Lights, and still farther the Land of the Thunder, and still farther the Land of the Rings, and still farther the old abolished Sky, and still farther the exterior Ocean, and still farther the Hell of Limits, and finally the Universe-Isles.

How to name the narrator?

You will call him the spy of distances.

IX. THE 53 STAGES OF THE TOKAIDO
OF HIROSHIGE

For Toru Shimizu

The journey toward Kyoto from the capital of the East has all the characteristics of an initiatory trip, with its temptations, tests, customs barriers, its fords, bridges, sounds of the sea, gorges, storms; but the apparent goal, the imperial city, appears nowhere in these engravings as a crowning stroke. We have the impression of one more stage, a rest longer than the others, after which one would need not to come back (the circumstances, the laws do oblige you to, however; one knows that the nobles had to reside in Tokyo one year out of two, and that the wives of the samurai could not leave it without special authorization), but to continue. It is not the fact of approaching Kyoto that brings us near paradise, it is the fact of going westward. And it is why, if one cannot move beyond this limit, one must perpetually begin the trip again, even if only in imagination and prints. These 53 stages are only the beginning of a dreamed-of journey (that is why the two outermost engravings do not enter into the count: they are there to orient the others), which would cause one to go outside Japan, to cross China or the ocean, would lead to the other side of the Earth. It is a question of departure for Europe, because the "famous sites" of this continent must be as useful as those of the archipelago in helping us imagine paradise.

It is the already celestial character that Japan can take on when one moves in it, and when it moves, that Hiroshige celebrates by making the most faithful nuances of the alleys, fields, rivers, and rocks play with layers of fabulous colors at the upper limits of his pictures. Because, if the sky if blue above the bridge of Nihombashi, it becomes orange above the sails of Shinagawa, then purple, vermilion, blackish-brown above the Oiso in the rain, iron grey above the ford of Odawara, pink, Prussian blue above the Numazu in the Moonlight, yellow ochre, ultramarine, charcoal grey above Kambara in the snow, orangy-pink, dark blue, citron yellow above the ford of Kanaya, violet above the bridge of Yokkaïchi in a gust of wind, etc. In several pictures the Earth climbs up to the sky; in three of them an object (Mount Fuji, a kite, a roadsign) breaks the upper frame, and in some, where the sky which is so important in the others appears absent at first sight, it is the paper of the margin itself which becomes celestial, as is particularly apparent in the 24th print, the ford of Shimada.

Among the nearby famous sites, authorized, there is one whose importance, if it had needed to be, comes from being brought back into prominence by Hokusaï. To rival Hokusaï was most of all to rival the 36 and 10 Views of Fuji. This double figure invited a continuation of the series: six of the Stages of the Tokaïdo are new Views, and in the 31st, when one is already so far away, the divine volcano seems to reappear: another mountain represents it. These six Other Views not only complete the work of Hokusaï but constitute a work within the work. This half-turn around the mountain is the figuration of a half-turn around the Earth, which calls for its complement. Around these six views are spread out the other stages, around which could be spread out also the celebrated views of the two capitals radiating around their two limits, and still hundreds more of other celebrated sites in the interior of Japan, then in the interior of the ancient world (China, India) and of the new which calls itself the West. If one could go not only all the way to Europe, but come back while continuing still toward the West (as today with planes which go via the pole) then, everything reversing itself (as, in the 15th print, Mount Fuji, instead of appearing as it does during the rest of the trip at the right of the traveler, passes sharply to his left), all Japan could appear like the figuration of paradise. For Hiroshige the Earth was round.

Nearly 40 times Hiroshige remade the 55 engravings of the Tokaïdo. We know that he took this route in 1831 or '32 to accompany the horses sent by the shogun of Tokyo to the emperor of Kyoto. Nothing says he made the trip again. The enormous success the first series had in no way explains why he spent a good part of the 20 some years of life remaining to him beginning it over, all the more because it is still this first version which has been the most in demand. He must have had the feeling of dying too soon, without having succeeded in offering 55 variations of the 55 engravings. Marching in order from east to west, they can be arranged beside each other as if cut from a single gigantic roll. Before dying Hiroshige wrote, "I leave my paintbrush in the east and go away to visit the famous sites of the west," which means: I am going to the paradise of the west, where Amida reigns, but also going from Tokyo toward Kyoto, which is a figuration of it, from the shogun toward the emperor, from present power, from its police and its administration, to the idealized power of rites and arts, from the Edo epoque not only toward the almost fabulous golden age of Heian but toward the open and dangerous effervescence of the Momoyama epoque. To the west of Kyoto, almost at the same distance, one makes out Nagasaki, that fissure through which filtered drop by drop, into the interior of the Japanese fortress, the novelties of the West, China evidently first, but especially this Far West which was then Europe. The first print, with its emphasized perspective, can be considered as a statement of principle.

X. MEDITATION ON THE FRONTIER

For Batuz

1) Limiting frontier

Snow, soot. Two countries: one covered with corn, the other with sunflowers, one pebbly, the other sandy. Here oak forests, there beech-trees. Two peoples: tall blonds with rosy complexions and blue eyes, little swarthy dark people with prominent cheekbones, slanting eyelids. The ones have an agglutinative language, the others an inflected one. Villages with roofs of tile or slate, or with roofs of thatch or slats. Clearings and migrations produce confrontations here and there, so much so that it is necessary to fix a division line, inscribe it, mark it out. There is perhaps a center there, the capital of an empire, that of a kingdom on the other side, from which come these radiations, these successive waves which break against this wall; but we concentrate our gaze on this region of the frontier where things would not be so different if there were not a whole tissue, a whole network of transmitting centers on both sides. The essential is that approaching this limit will unavoidably provoke unrest. It is fine for those in the distant medullary regions not to know this other, which we are confronted with daily, to behave as if it did not exist; we who live close to the barriers are always obliged to define ourselves in relation to the other.

2) Menacing frontier

When sunflowers or beechtrees stretch out all around, one can believe they are the only species of their kind; they do not raise questions. It is needless to defend them and one can amuse oneself in the botanical gardens, looking at exotic flowers and essences, extravagances to relax us. But when beyond the valley we suddenly perceive the forbidden oaks or the foreign grains, we know there is a menace there, that their seeds may win out. Thus our beechtrees are not only beechtrees, but anti-oaks; thus the roofs of our villages perpetually proclaim the eulogies of tile against thatch, or shingle against slate. In our consciousness, the other is always there.

3) Intimate frontier

We are double: the frontier passes through the middle of our heart; and, however, we are of one side or of the other, one part of ourselves for centuries represses the other, wants to prevent its expressing itself, to cover it up, to devour it. The hatred for the one who lives on the other side of the water comes from the fact that his voice is never silent on this side. Thus at the approach toward the frontier, all that was calm in the great plains is agitated and sharpened.

4) Spectral frontier

If the line were very straight, everything would perhaps calm down. Ignorance could win out in the long run; the other would become invisible. The frontier would become the end of the world. But the least irregularity, the least fissure, suffices for tensions to be established not only perpendicularly to the frontier but along it; a hollow here to which replies opposite not only a hump, but an inverse hollow a little farther, and so forth. Each of these uneven places will reecho in currents and vibrations. If the territory the frontier runs along takes on a color, a life, a consciousness different from that which is found where it is surrounded by territories similar to itself, what will happen to the one that is encircled by it on almost all sides? Or to the one in which the frontier, like a weapon, penetrates, and whose sharpened end is obliged to reinforce itself, extending into the interior of our domains, like a planned frontier, a desire to separate us? Some particularity of the terrain will give an advantage to some kind of vegetation, custom, language. A little farther it is another feature that will be decisive; and all that will even itself out little by little in a relatively stable track, which will consitute, so to speak, the differential benefit between these two regions of our earth and of our soul: Austria and Hungary.

5) Deep frontier

To concentrate in painting on the phenomenon of the frontier, it is indispensable to eliminate as much as possible the other edges of our representation. This is why the works will never be big enough. We will have to be able to thrust ourselves in, to engulf ourselves in the contemplation of a given region, live in it as if it did not have a frontier, to be able then to approach it, to see it work. This is why, by conserving a grossly rectangular form, exactly because in being traditional this does not draw attention to itself, we take away from it all stiffness. Even squaring the linen canvas, traditional support of this art, would give too much emphasis to the frame. This is why we will constitute little by little a territory, by successive alluvial deposits, with a material which we will choose specially as a long-time carrier of information, leaving sometimes the possibility of still deciphering some "news" from yesteryear, all papers, from newspapers to cardboard, imitating thus the process of Nature and of History, which will have the advantage of furnishing us with a sort of deep expanse, a time trap: felt, thatch, bark, in the interior of which the rumblings of flux and reflux will have every opportunity to express themselves, the advantage also of blotting, of imprinting in some way the exterior space, the encounter with which could sometimes still be softened through the transition of a frame of the same material, of the same nature, before the official frame permitting this foreign picture, this icon of the presence of the foreigner, to be hung.

6) Natural frontier

In this alchemical treatment, the paper is purified to become a support for the meditation on our own intimate frontiers, to furnish light on our intestinal wars, and for that, through that, unveils its own history, its origins: it becomes tattered into fibers which will link up the different points of the territory like those packets of wires of all colors in the compartments of electronic brains, or the neurons of our nervous system, and acknowledges its vegetable origin so well that it is possible to pass almost without noticing to straw, to grass, to lichen. The image material thus obtained becomes like a natural event and reacts to the light of the passing day like a meadow, a carpet of dead leaves in the undergrowth, or a rock covered with mosses. One can even imagine, rejoining certain fulgurations of the gardeners of the Far East, a manifesto work made of live grass, or more exactly of a drying of grass in the middle of a meadow, leaving a frontier of flowers. Always at ease among the trees, the icon becomes here a resume of the History of the World, meditation on the frontier which separates nature and culture.

7) Free frontier

The habits of our language make us place ourselves to the right of the frontier. The left will be the other, sometimes the sinister, often the limitless. The line is more of a frontier on its right side than on its left, and that is natural, whatever may be the real geographic position of the peoples who can serve as a concrete application in our meditation. Thus, while Austria with its mountains, monasteries, and string quartets, is to the West, Hungary with its immense spaces, its great lakes with marshy shores peopled with reeds always shaken by a wind one would think from central Asia, its troops of wild horses preserving in their manes the memory of conquering migrations of their ancestors until the establishment of a sufficiently solid frontier which has reorganized everything, corresponds to it on the East; but we need only place ourselves in the North to reestablish the habitual semantic situation. When we pass over to the American continent, whether North or South, in the United States or in Argentina, the figure applies with all its force without transposition. It is really the right or the East which is organized, centralizing, and more or less centralized, which devours little by little a more and more distant West, which is on the other side of this moving, particularly alive, and enriching frontier, that which had no frontiers, the country of wandering and even of permissiveness, the place of breathing far from worn-out codes, even though a more thorough examination obliges one to moderate all that considerably.

8) Constitutive frontier

Opposition between a centered region and one not centered, or much less so; one could wonder what permits a frontier to constitute itself in opposition to the progressive radiation of such a center. The study of incomplete frontiers shows us that it is partly appropriate to invert things: the progressive radiation of a growing center to the right encounters often fortuitous resistances in what was formerly without frontiers, which resistances organize themselves into multiple centers of opposition. One can say that any interruption of the flux, of the primitive migration, even due to accidental causes, will provoke a sort of analysis or dialysis, will separate little by little into two distinct populations that which was at first only a single settlement. This frontier is originally a dotted line, as our geographical maps show us so well, and the examination of each of its fragments permits us to learn how, in times of crisis, when the menace of the other becomes particularly alarming, they will have a tendency to rejoin and reinforce each other.

9) Thick frontier

It is especially when the center itself feels itself threatened that it will reinforce its frontier, will make a great wall of it, more and more impervious, more and more towering, trying to intercept even the flight of birds and radio broadcasts. The more the frontier in the beginning is accidental, decided for example by a distant center, headquarters, or an international meeting, with no consultation with those involved, the more it has a tendency to become evil, bristling, murderous (Berlin Wall, 32nd Parallel); it will then cast its shadow over the surrounding regions. At its maximum of defiance, the frontier doubles itself inevitably into two lines, each turned toward the exterior, but which must also protect the interior against the threat not only of the other but also of this intermediary interstitial region, the no-man's-land, this geographical expression of misunderstanding, of rift, at first a corridor of death, desolation, and barbed wire, but which can sometimes soften and become the very image of the crossing of frontiers when that finally begins to occur.

10) Crossed frontier

The very marking out of the frontier constituted an analysis of the differences between territories, among people. With these thick and redoubled frontiers, projections on the horizontal plane of their vertical reinforcements, we reach the expression of what questions them, of what will pass beyond and fly over them. If the frontier becomes more dense, this is indeed because it is more and more difficult to maintain it; it is because more and more on both sides people want it to be crossed; more and more the frontiersman is conscious not only of the existence of the other, but of his virtues; more and more he wants to know him, rebelling thus against the injunctions of the center or of the right, who wish to close all the remaining openings with the intention moreover of protecting this frontiersman himself against the unimaginable dangers of the other. It is because the consciousness of the center inhabitant does not have the same structure. The more the walls are raised, the more the headquarters trembles, but the more the watchmen plunge into the landscapes of the other side, which fascinate them more and more.

11) Open frontier

Happily, little by little all territories touch each other on some border. The airplane introduces the customs and police formalities into the suburbs of the capitals. We all become frontiersmen. Left and right clasp hands. It is thus that the frontiers which for a long time were the most impenetrable slowly become transparent; the intermediary regions, the regions of passage, the doors, the interstices become new centers (Hong Kong, Singapore, the Rivieras) toward which crowds converge and from which they spread out, instructed in a new way to listen to things.

12) Livable frontier

Thus the overcome frontier becomes a vibrating membrane, that which produces the sound as well as that which receives it. It becomes the place where two territories press together lovingly, the contact point of their two skins. The redoubled frontier, freed, comes to life as a couple who dance, drawing their shadow and their flame on the walls of the cave Earth and conquering space in their embraces.

XI. DISTANT COMEDY

For Jennifer Waelti-Walters

The imaginary invalid arrives in Naples. There he encounters the flying doctor who presents him to the Grand Turk. The latter, charmed, makes him a gift of an elixir which, when taken, causes a thick curly dark purple fleece to grow all over his body, which disturbs him somewhat. But the flying doctor succeeds in shaving it off fairly cleanly in order to have it spun and woven by his wife into a banner which the Grand Turk needs for his flagship. Argan's skin becomes then soft, warm, luminous as copper, and he finds himself in excellent health in all the vigor of his twenty years. The daughter of the Grand Turk, who was watching the scene behind a scroll-cut screen, wants him then in marriage, and her father is enchanted. It has to be said that Béline had just died during the voyage, stifled by her own venom. The funeral was simple and the tears discreet. Two persons of great beauty, representing music and dance, then execute a little divertissement during which they go to find Louison, all grown up, whom they crown with jasmine.

*
* *

The learned ladies having just heard that the National Library is in flames rush to the Rue de Richelieu to offer their assistance to the firemen, who are completely overwhelmed by the event. Then rushes forth from a boulevard a troop of very well-trained monkeys, whom they have succeeded in teaching to speak. After several incantations and variously delightful masquerades they put out the fire, but the ladies walking in the devastated galleries cannot hold back their tears. The monkeys then go looking in the garrets of the surrounding streets for some young avant-garde writers, who ask nothing better than to rewrite the lost books and to console them in every way.

*
* *

Don Juan this time disguises himself as the minotaur, and Sganarelle as a ship's captain. After a perilous voyage they reach America, where they are welcomed by naked warriors crowned with feathers, who marvel at the attire of the two companions and Don Juan's head. They have them pass in a great procession down the streets of a splendid city planted with palm and lemon trees, to present them to the king, who remembers that in his childhood a sorceror-teacher had told him about a race of heifers with human faces who lived on an island in the other ocean. They organize an expedition, but it is naturally Sganarelle who falls in love with the princess Pasiphaé, whom he marries to the sound of fifes and lutes. As for Don Juan, more and more proud of his horns and his muzzle, because the mask has now become skin, he sets out again for other labyrinths.

*

* *

At the school for wives Agnes forgets her handkerchief. At the school for husbands Cléante discovers a kitten. This is nothing other than Puss in Boots dressed up in children's clothes. Slipping into the school for wives, he brings back a handkerchief, which he places in Agnes's lap. Her father is a terrible ogre who would like to eat Cléante and the cat, but the latter then takes on the shape of the wife whom the monster had lost and who was as compassionate as she was beautiful. The ogre lets himself be moved, and it all ends with a double marriage to which all the students of the school for cats are invited.

*

* *

The bourgeois gentleman wants absolutely to marry off the daughter of the music teacher to the son of the dance teacher, but the latter is hopelessly in love with the daughter of the philosophy teacher, who is himself tenderly smitten by the sister of the fencing teacher. In the course of a divertissement given by Madame Jourdain in honor of her 30th wedding anniversary, where one sees a great number of violins and oboes from Poitou disguised as animals from the Indies, one discovers that the music teacher's daughter is in reality the dance teacher's, who had been stolen by gypsies at an early age and taken in by her supposed father. Mr. Jourdain then does everything possible to facilitate her marriage with the master tailor, who furnishes new suits for the whole company.

*

* *

As a result of double-dealing, Scapin finds himself in the galleys, a new theatre for his exploits. He does not delay in captivating the son of the captain, who has seen in a Barbary ship two eyes he cannot erase from his memory. From oarsman, Scapin becomes a cook and persuades the father to entertain the one who is holding this interesting captive. When the invitation is returned, Scapin ransacks the basements, but the beautiful eyes are not to be found. As a precaution, the young lady had been confided to a neighboring pasha, who keeps her in a white citadel above the rocks and the whirlwinds. Scapin succeeds in bringing about a naval battle in order to be taken prisoner. When the pasha comes back to visit the cells in the foundations of his hanging gardens, he recognizes an amulet on the chest of the mischievous galley-slave. It is his son, whom he had lost during a shipwreck somewhere near Stromboli! Scapin does not hesitate a moment to become Moslem in order to collect his inheritance. Rejoicing in the mosque with tambourines and sweets. The daughter becomes a Christian. Carillons, organs and fanfares, parade of wedding gifts with royal benediction. A great celebration in the manner of Versailles to end up.

*

* *

Tartuffe has just confided Orgon's money-box to Harpagon. The miser cannot keep himself from forcing the lock, but he finds no coins in it, only tiny frog-sized monkeys, dressed in delightfully tight-fitting silk suits, who offer him a thousand services, but he will have to pay for everything. Harpagon falls sick over it. The little monkeys transform themselves into doctors and pleasantly administer to him all sorts of potions and treatments, which make him sicker still. When he finally offers them his whole fortune to cure him, they reveal to him that they are under the command of Damis, who has become a powerful magician on his return from adventures in the Orient. It is he who persuaded Orgon to allow the money-box to be stolen by the hypocrite, whose crimes Damis had revealed to him in order to deliver Uncle Harpagon from his deplorable stinginess. A blue mirror from Travancore had showed him in advance the unfolding of all these scenes. Tartuffe arrives, sees himself lost, kneels, wrings his hands, bursts into tears, and succeeds in getting Marianne to weaken, and she intercedes in his favor. They allow him to sail for the Antilles. Delighted with the country he discovers, he makes an honest fortune there without using the least slave, and has everyone come over. Harpagan pays for fitting out the ship. The monkeys are changed into fish, and Damis leaves for the conquest of the daughter of the King of the Waves.

*
* *

Alceste is traveling. He has decided to flee French society. He learns languages. He experiences the discomforts of inns and ships. Soon his fortune has melted away. He then lives true adventures, becomes a sailor, is promoted rapidly because of his courage and his wit, but his vessel encounters pirates and he is stranded on the Turkish shore. There he is rowing in the galleys of the Great Lord. He falls overboard during a battle in the Persian Gulf, succeeds in escaping, is rescued by a Dutch ship en route to Japan. He gets enthusiastic over calligraphy and becomes a venerated master.

XII. SONGS OF THE ROSE OF VOICES

For Henri Pousseur

The troubadour of Flanders, toward the North:
  These are litanies of honey
  Honey is the amber of forests
  Honey is the crystal of flowers
  Honey is blond like women
  It is the balm for our miseries
  Get me rays of honey
  I shall love you all my life

Goethe at Frankfort, toward the East:
  The world reveals to my soul
  The energy of its creation
  Are they traced by a divine hand
  These characters which unveil
  The mysteries of Nature
  Get up and go bathe
  Among the caresses of the dawn

William Blake at London, farther toward the North:
  In a printing press of hell
  I have learned by what methods
  Knowledge is transmitted
  Lions of fire raging around
  Melt metals into dew
  Then give them forms of books
  Which they melt into libraries

The sorceror of Iaroslav, farther toward the East:
  The phoenix in my empire
  Weaves a nest in the black night
  And sets it on fire and burns himself up also
  The river Eden in my empire
  Bathes the empress stone

Dante in Florence, toward the South:
    Golden heart of celestial rose
    Blossoming out in perfume
    Toward a forever dawning spring
    If your beginning already harvests
    As many torches as splendors
    They will ripen at the ultimate points

The Viking Iceland-bound, again toward the North:
    Way down below the serpent coils
    Biting his tail around the world
    The giants try climbing
    By the rainbow which falls into ruins
    The ocean covers up the Earth
    No more Sun stars rain down

John at Patmos, again toward the East:
    The twelve doors of the city
    Each formed of a pearl
    Remain always wide open
    Because there will be no more night
    On the squares of transparent gold
    The phantoms of the ancient temples
    Smile at the luminous nations
    Which circulate their treasures

Aeschylus at Athens, farther toward the South:
    Men were blind
    Until the day when we taught them
    The science of the journey of the stars
    We put wings of canvas
    On the ships to explore
    And as reward for our discoveries
    The jealous chained us

Hugo at Guernesey, toward the West:
    Everything seeks everything without respite or cessation

Mud rises up toward heaven
The ardent faun tree and caves
Are filled with immense sighs

The Eskimo witch-doctor at Rasmussen, very far to the North:
If you knew oh strangers
The terror which sometimes
We feel you would understand
Why we love festivals
Songs, music and dance

The troubadour of Flanders comes to accompany him:
And the honey amber of the forests

Tchouang-Tseu in his hermitage, very far to the East:
Seem a body but am not one
Day and fire reveal me
I dissolve in the shadows

Goethe comes to accompany him:
And the world then uncovers to me
The swarming of its life

Firdousi at Ispahan, again toward the South:
Without you delight of my soul
The entire universe is nothing to me
You make all my deserts flower
Soaring above the stars
You outshine the Sun
You change the world into a caress

Cervantes at Salamanca, farther toward the West:
The lame have left their crutches
Cadavers have left their shrouds
All resurrected healthy and free
In the time of mercy

The monk of Kyoto, among the islands of the North-East:
    Impermanence leads us
    To leave this celestial palace
    To go visit men

William Blake comes to accompany him:
    In a printing press of hell
    We will publish our failures

Then the viking:
    Serpents biting our own napes
    In the midst of lamentations

Quartet of eagles:
    All the energy of the phoenixes
    In the calligraphed empire
    Comes together at the pearls of the city
    Which flower from twelve doors

The praise-singer Kabyle, very far to the South:
    When the boy begins to beat
    The drum the house begins
    To rock when he beats
    And sings with all his force
    The house bounds into the air

Dante comes to accompany him:
    At the heart of the rose of voices

The Breton minstrel, again toward the West:
    Twelve signs for twelve months
    The next to the last Sagittarius
    Lets fly his arrow the blood
    Flows in streams the trumpet sounds
    Fire and thunder rain and wind
    Nothing nothing more no other series

Quartet of angels:
>Crystal knowledge of flowers
>Honey of generations transmitted
>In the depths the serpent
>Coils among terror

The pilgrim at the Ganges, among the vines of the South-East:
>Next to a woman who sings
>Red black white is stretched out
>A male he too a singer
>Who enjoys her while still singing

The sorceror comes to accompany him:
>And weaves them a nest in the night

Then Tchouang-Tseu:
>Smaller and greater than everything

The pilgrim resumes:
>Their two bodies are of transparent gold

Hugo joins in:
>Faun tree enjoying the sky

Quartet of bulls:
>In the springtime always birth
>I taught them the science
>Of trajectories of houses
>Thus when the boy begins
>To beat the drum the stars
>Begin to rock
>Dragging along the deserts of the sky

Melville at New Bedford, very far toward the West:
>Although whiteness is the symbol
>Of a merciful power
>And the robes of the lovers

Are white like virgin wool
He prowls in the depths of whiteness

Hugo comes to accompany him:
Without respite cessation or rest

Melville resumes:
An elusive principle which strikes
The soul with a panic terror

Arrow of dolphins:
By the rainbow which falls into ruins
The ice giants come back
Bringing a glimmer of honey
Which burns them and kisses them
The fire being like women
You will understand oh strangers
That impermanence makes us
Set fire to the celestial palaces

The Aztec at Sahagun, among the scalps of the Southwest:
A very long time ago the gods
Having met asked
Who was going to govern men

Aeschylus comes to accompany him:
Because they do everything backward

The Aztec resumes:
Who should serve them as Sun

Firdousi comes to accompany him:
Without whom delight of our souls
The whole world is nothing to us

The Aztec:
But when this sun was born

The gods felt themselves die

Quartet of lions:
>The mud wishes to mark the white
>Among the twelve blind signs
>Because under the royalty of white
>Eyes and hands are at war

Arrow of serpents:
>All the doors are open
>All the ships have wings
>The characters unveil to us
>The living forces of Nature
>In full day we stretch out
>Next to a woman who sings
>Red white black and gold

The Indian from the Island of Vancouver among the fogs of the North-West:
>The sea is an immense river
>Which rustles toward the North-West

Cervantes comes to accompany him:
>Where opens up among the crutches
>Which the lame have laid down

The Indian resumes:
>The entrance to the underground world
>Of the dead when the tide goes out
>In the twilights of the moons
>Closes up when it comes in again

The minstrel comes to accompany him:
>Signs letting fly their darts

Echo from the Antipodes:
>Get up and go bathe

In the honey balm of miseries
If your beginnings already harvest
As many torches as desires
They will ripen on your faun trees
In caves full of signs

Arrow of salamanders:
Gravitating higher than roses
Shrouds which the dead throw off
How many splendors you will ripen
If the boy beats hard enough
When the houses rise up

Arrow of dragons:
Sound flows with fire and blood
The chorus of lions descends from the sky
In clothing of white sighs
Into the caves of the oceans
Which the tide of flames invades

Octet of wings:
Right in the middle of our empire
Metals melt in drunkenness
Lavas sing on the fields
Temples change into ships
With transparent wings
Spin along on oceans of honey
To capture the spirit of thunder
Son of the Sun of rain and wind
All resurrected healthy and free

Octet of hands:
If we love festivals and dances
Which govern our universe
Male festivals female dances
In the whitenesses of our shadows
Let us multiply the joys

In the beatings of our voices
Climbing back up immense rivers
To be reborn at the abode of the gods

Octet of eyes:
  Get us rays of honey
  To make our bodies transparent
  In the shadows of whiteness
  Blossoming out in perfumes
  In the pearl of nights without night
  Without truce cessation or rest
  Festivals beatings songs and dances
  The bounding of the houses

Motet for twelve:
  Transmutations of the failures
  Reversals of royalties
  Empires of mercies
  Immensity of the smallest
  Crowding in the most empty
  And emptiness in the heart of the thickest
  We give it the form of books
  And at the moment when the sentence is born
  The stars fall into ruins
  In the river Eden where bathes
  Escarboucle queen of the dead
  Nations tremble at her voice
  Groans of deliverance

Madrigal for twenty:
  I shall love you all my life
  Sovereign of all roses
  Of fire of thunder and of wind
  Who bounds across the night
  In the purple of our shadows
  In the chain of our sighs
  In the panic of our lives

Where the stars weep for their cycles
Ultimate rose of our voices
If we wanted all strangers
Peoples of all countries
To distill for it our silence
The lamentations of our skies
The disappearances of our gods
The trees of our ancestry
The decisions of our phantoms
In the light of echos
In a sign of transparency
We would bid one another farewell
For the sentence of our loves

Fourth Part
POSTSCRIPT

Dear Christian Jacomino:

I'm taking advantage of the space you have left me at the end of your book to take stock of my projects a little. When this text appears, *A Thousand and One Folds* will have seen the light at Gallimard: with this work, the series *Stuff of Dreams* will be finished. The series *Repertory* is also concluded, but there are others in the works, for example, *Improvisations,* in which I'm trying to bring together the essence of my courses at the University of Geneva and others. It began with the *Improvisations on Flaubert* with Différence Publishers; those on *Henri Michaux* have just come out at Fata Morgana Publishers. All my public courses are taped. I've had a certain number of them transcribed, which gives me a large collection already. The first ones I'll transcribe and revise now will be those on *Rimbaud,* probably during the summer of '86; then will come those on *Artaud* (summer '88?), probably finally those on *Molière* (summer of '90?). From now on I can't put the finishing touches on a volume except in summer.

It's probable that I'll stop there, because I don't intend to go beyond the number five here either. I'll perhaps find another idea for using at least some scraps of the rest and of courses that I'll have given from now until then. I'll probably have succeeded in winding up *Illustrations* with the fifth of the series, which ought especially to include various excerpts from the *Song for Don Juan* and to advance further that of *Envoys* with the third, *Extra,* and perhaps even the fourth, *Reserve,* but that would surprise me, because although I already have much too much material, I still have to choose, arrange, edit an explanatory note for each piece selected, and that takes an awful lot of time. We shall see.

But the big job for the moment is *Transit,* the fourth *Spirit of the Place,* in which I intend to put *Saga, The Parliament of Idols, Floatings from East to West,* from which comes the piece on Hiroshige, *The Vision of Namur,* from which come the *Songs of the Rose of Voices, Elsinore,* and *Windows on the Inner Passage,* from which comes *Distant Comedy,* texts all already published here and there, but for which I hope to have succeeded in editing in this summer of '85 a somewhat fantastic tale of my trip to Mexico, which has already been waiting to be edited for some years. Then it, too, will appear in all probability first in isolated fashion, as a sort of little novel, before I combine it with others in some way I'm not yet too certain of. One of my principal problems with this book is to maintain it within reasonable proportions, because the present state of French publishing prevents such sumptuous productions as that of *Boomerang* for years to come.

All this will appear then when it can, as it can, and brings us at least up to 1991. It's necessary first of all to get there. I'll then be 65 years old. That's the age for retirement. How many best-sellers will be forgotten between now and then! How many bankruptcies? How many new fads in painting! How many changes of government! I don't even mention all that which we don't imagine, all that which we imagine without wanting to say it, without daring, the worst and perhaps also the best. One can always, one must always dream. Something in any case will have been carried on beneath the waves.

But let's act as if we were going to discuss the last *Spirit of the Place,* the last *Envoys,* whatever, knock on wood, will have blossomed from now until then, already started up in this last decade until the year 2000, turning point for what?

"Credette Cimabue nella pintura
Tener lo campo, e ora ha Giotto il grido.
Si che la fama di colui è scura.

Costi ha tolto l'uno a l'altro Guido
La gloria della lingua; e forse è nato
Chi l'uno e l'altro caccerà del nido."
Dante, *Purgatory*

"Cimabue thought he dominated the field
In painting; the popularity of Giotto
Overshadowed him.

As for poetry Guido Cavalcanti
Replaced Guido Guinicelli
Just until a new one comes to dislodge them."

Let's come back to '85 to glance briefly at this "as if," to comment a little on the how of this broadcasting expression, because outside and before these normal editions—which are constituted little by little into complete works, which, you see, are always in some respect incomplete, the finishing of such a series accentuating the opening of others and of the whole—there is a whole progressive unveiling, all a bubbling and scribbling.

Things present themselves today in the following manner, and I admit I have more and more difficulty in controlling them, which is, however, essential, because the vigor and depth feel the effects of it if one lets oneself go too much (the quantity hardly counts; from the point of view of mass I have already published only too much, and it's necessary to change gears). There are roughly four stages. First, the appearance of the solicitation, the occasion of the text: catalogue of an exhibit, *de luxe* book, unavoidable participation in a given ceremony or homage, the release of the essay. Then there are the reprintings in journals. Then come the first reassemblings into a collection with young, marginal, provincial, foreign editors, before the more or less definitive arrangement, which almost rids me of it, which did rid me of it better a few years ago, because the very form of these texts composed of retrievable and mobile elements at several levels makes them function for me today like a sort of attic, more and more spacious, in which new possibilities for combination, new adventures, turn over and over. There the texts go to sleep, but they dream.

Picasso said—I don't remember when and I don't remember where—that he had built himself a solitude equal to any test. Thus I enjoy in my nook a perilous liberty, and the issue is to make it last, because I still feel I have enough to do for a hundred years. It's a question of sharing it so that it will last, outside me as in me, on all sides of my frontier, of the porous frontier that I am, afterwards, for example. What is certain is that you help me in this, like all those who will have read me, thanks to you.

Michel BUTOR

Fifth Part
ESSENTIAL
BIBLIOGRAPHY

NOVELS, AUTOBIOGRAPHY

Milan Passage [*Passage de Milan*]. Paris: Minuit, 1954. Published by 10/18, 1970.

Time Schedule [*Emploi du temps*]. Paris: Minuit, 1956. Published by 10/18, 1966, followed by "The Example," by Georges Raillard.

Change of Heart [*La Modification*]. Paris: Minuit, 1957. Published by 10/18, 1962, followed by "Mythological Realism of M. B.," by Michel Leiris.

Degrees [*Degrés*]. Paris: Gallimard, Collection Blanche, 1960. Published in Collection Imaginaire, 1978, with cover text by Michel Sicard.

Portrait of the Artist as a Young Monkey [*Portrait de l'artiste en jeune singe*]. Paris: Gallimard, 1967.

Interlude [*Intervalle*]. Paris: Gallimard, 1973.

STEREOPHONIC STUDIES, ACCOUNTS OF DREAMS AND OF TRAVEL

Mobile [*Mobile*]. Paris: Gallimard, 1962.

Airline Network [*Réseau aérien*]. Paris: Gallimard, 1962.

Description of St. Mark's [*Description de San Marco*]. Paris: Gallimard, 1963.

6,810,000 Liters of Water a Second [*6.810.000 litres d'eau par seconde*]. Paris: Gallimard, 1965.

Spirit of the Place [*Le génie du lieu*]. Paris: Grasset, 1958.

Where/Or (Spirit of the Place 2) [*Où (Le Génie du lieu 2)*]. Paris: Gallimard, 1971.

Boomerang [*Boomerang*]. Paris: Gallimard, 1978.

The Rose of the Winds (32 Rhumbs for Charles Fourier) [*La Rose des vents (32 Rhumbs pour Charles Fourier)*]. Paris: Gallimard, 1970.

Dialogue with 33 variations of L. V. Beethoven on a Waltz of Diabelli [*Dialogue avec 33 variations de L. V. Beethoven sur une valse de Diabelli*]. Paris: Gallimard, 1971.

Stuff of Dreams [*Matière de rêves*]. Paris: Gallimard, Collection Le Chemin, 1975.

Second Basement [*Second sous-sol; Matière de rêves 2*]. Paris: Gallimard, Le Chemin, 1976.
Third Cellar [*Troisième dessous; Matière de rêves 3*]. Paris: Gallimard, Le Chemin, 1977.
Quadrupled Base [*Quadruple fond; Matière de rêves 4*]. Paris: Gallimard, Le Chemin, 1981.
A Thousand and One Folds [*Mille et un plis; Matière de rêves 5*]. Paris: Gallimard, Le Chemin, 1985.

POETRY, OPERA LIBRETTI

The Suburb from Dawn to Sunrise [*La banlieue de l'aube à l'aurore*], followed by *Brownian Movement* [*Mouvement brownien*]. Montpellier: Fata Morgana, 1968.
Approach Works [*Travaux d'approche*]. Paris: Gallimard, Collection Poche/Poésie, 1972.
Don Juan in the Channel [*Don Juan dans la Manche*]. Paris: Obliques, special issue, 1975.
Window on the Inner Passage [*Fenêtre sur le passage intérieur*]. Ancrages: "Bois de Champ," 1982. Audiocassette, Paris: Artalect, 1983.

On the basis of visual or sound images:

Illustrations [*Illustrations*]. Paris: Gallimard, Le Chemin, 1964.
Illustrations II. Paris: Gallimard, 1969.
Illustrations III. Paris: Gallimard, Le Chemin, 1973.
Illustrations IV. Paris: Gallimard, Le Chemin, 1976.
Envoys [*Envois*]. Paris: Gallimard, Le Chemin, 1980.
Armful of April [*Brassée d'avril*]. Paris: La Différence, Collection La Fêlure, 1982.
Express [*Exprès; Envois 2*]. Paris: Gallimard, Le Chemin, 1983.
Foretaste [*Avant-goût*]. Rennes: Ubacs, 1984.
Lunar Herbarium [*Herbier lunaire*]. Paris: La Différence, 1984.
The Dog King [*Le Chien Roi*]. Paris: Daniel Lelong, 1984.
Men at Work [*Chantier*]. Gourdon: Dominique Bedou, 1985.

Opera libretti, discography:

Landscape of Response [*Paysage de répons*] followed by *Dialogue of the Reigns* [*Dialogue des règnes*]. Alveuve: Castella, 1968.
Your Faust [*Votre Faust*], with Henri Pousseur:
—Paris: Notebooks of the Center for Marxist Study and Research, produced by J.-Y. Bosseur, Diffusion-Odéon, 1968.
—Reggio Calabria: Alba Pellegrino Ceccarelli, Edizioni Parallelo 38, French and Italian translation, 1977.
—Freiburg: original music album, 3 records, Harmonia Mundi, 1973.
Matter for a Don Juan [*Matériel pour un Don Juan*], matrix of *A Song for Don Juan* [*Une Chanson pour Don Juan*], audiocassette by Jean-Yves Bosseur with *Don Juan in the Orchestra* [*Don Juan dans l'orchestre*] with the voice of Michel Butor. Losne: La louve de l'hiver, 1977.
The Dream of Irenaeus [*Le rêve d'Irénée*], libretto and audiocassette. Chatillon-sous-Bagneux: Ed. Cercles, Collection "Sontexte," 1979.
Elsinore [*Elseneur*] with René Koering. Volumen, 1979; and Paris: Radio-France, 1980.
Tresses of Time [*Chevelures du temps*] with Henri Pousseur. Conservatoire de Liège, 1980.
The Vision of Namur, Intended for the Rose of Voices [*La vision de Namur, à l'intention de la rose des voix*] with Henri Pousseur. Lausanne: La Thiele, Collection Modulation, 1983.

LITERARY CRITICISM

Repertory I [*Repertoire I*]. Studies on "The Novel as Research," John Donne, Racine, Mme de Lafayette, Balzac, Kierkegaard, Baudelaire, Dostoievsky, Jules Verne, Proust, Roussel, Joyce, Ezra Pound, Faulkner, Leiris. Paris: Minuit, 1960.
Essays on the Moderns [*Essais sur les modernes*]. This volume contains the principal studies on the authors explored in *Repertory I* and *II*. Paris: Gallimard, Collection Idées, 1971.
Repertory II. Studies on Rabelais, Cervantes, Laclos, Chateaubriand, Hugo, Mallarmé, Proust. . . and "The Novel and Poetry," "The Use of

Personal Pronouns in the Novel," "The Individual and the Group. . ." etc., theoretical topics recollected in *Essays on the Novel*. Paris: Minuit, 1964.

Essays on the Novel [*Essais sur le roman*]. Paris: Gallimard, Collection Idées, 1972.

Repertory III. Studies on "Criticism and Invention," "Archeology," "Opera," and on Holbein, Caravaggio, Rousseau, Diderot, Hokusai, Hugo, Monet, Picasso, Mondrian, Rothko. . . Paris: Minuit, 1968.

Repertory IV. Studies on "Travel and Writing," "Words in Painting," "Mode and Modern," and on Villon, Rabelais, Fourier, Flaubert, Baudelaire, Lautréamont, Zola, Proust, Max Ernst, Barthes. . . Paris: Minuit, 1974.

Repertory V. Studies: "Where Do You Get That," "Literature and the Night," "Utopia," "Don Juan. . ." and on Rabelais, Dürer, Perrault, Beethoven, Stendhal, Proust, Mondrian, Dotremont. Paris: Minuit, 1982.

Essays on the Essays [*Essais sur les essais*]. Study on Montaigne. Paris: Gallimard, 1968.

Extraordinary Tale (Essay on a Dream of Baudelaire) [*Histoire extra-ordinaire (essai sur un rêve de Baudelaire*]. Paris: Gallimard, 1962.

Improvisations on Flaubert [*Improvisations sur Flaubert*]. Paris: La Différence, 1984.

Improvisations on Henri Michaux. Montpellier: Fata Morgana, 1985.

Dialogues:

Conversations with Michel Butor [*Entretiens avec Michel Butor*], by Georges Charbonnier. Paris: Gallimard, 1967.

M. B. Traveller at the Wheel [*M. B. voyageur à la roue*], with Jean-Marie le Sidaner. Paris: Ed. Encre, Collection Brèches, 1979.

Vanity (Conversation in the Maritime Alps) [*Vanité (conversation dans les Alpes Maritimes)*]. Paris: Balland, "Le commerce des idées," 1980.

Resistances [*Résistances*], with Michel Launey. Paris: Presse universitaire française, Collection "Ecriture," 1983.

*A Voyage with M. B., * [*Voyage avec M. B.*], with Madeleine Santschi. Lausanne: l'Age d'homme, 1983.

Translation:

Of the Origin of the Gods [*De l'origine des dieux*], by B. De Sahagun, translated into French by M. B. Montpellier: Fata Morgana, 1981.

ART CRITICISM, ART BOOKS:

Jacques Hérold. Paris: Georges Fall, "Le Musée de Poche," 1964.
Words in Painting [*Les Mots dans la peinture*]. Geneva: Skira, "Les Sentiers de la création," 1969.
Repertory [*Répertoire*], on Peverelli. Montpellier: Fata Morgana, 1972.
Butor/Masurovsky, manuscript engravings. Obliques, special issue, 1976.
The Little Mirrors [*Les Petits miroirs*]. Text for children illustrated by Gregory Masurovsky. Paris: La Farandole, 1972.
The Shipwrecked of the Arc [*Les Naufragés de l'Arche*]. Photographs from the Museum of Natural History, by Pierre Béranger. Paris: La Différence, 1982.
Sixteen and One Variations of Albert Ayme [*Seize et une variations d'Albert Ayme*], with Dominique and Jean-Yves Bosseur. Paris: Traversière, 1983.
Vieira da Silva. Paris: La Différence, "L'autre Musée," 1983.

In Collaboration with Michel Sicard:

Dotremont and his Writing-Engravings [*Dotremont et ses écrivures*]. Paris: Jean-Michel Place, 1978.
Staritsky, Materials and Talismans [*Staritsky, matières et talismans*]. Paris: Jean-Michel Place, 1978.
Problems in Contemporary Art Based on the Works of Henri Maccheroni [*Problèmes de l'art contemporain à partir des travaux d'Henri Maccheroni*]. Paris: Bourgois, 1983.
Alechinsky: Frontiers and Borders [*Alechinsky: frontières et bordures*]. Paris: Galilée, Collection Renault Art et Industrie, 1984.
Alechinsky in the Text [*Alechinsky dans le texte*]. Paris: Galilée, 1984.

CRITICAL BIBLIOGRAPHY

We give here only some basic books entirely consecrated to M. B.

Jean Roudaut, *Michel Butor or the Future Book* [*M. B. ou le Livre futur*]. Paris: Gallimard, Collection "Le Chemin," 1964.

Georges Raillard, *Butor*. Paris: Gallimard, Collection "La Bibliothèque idéale," 1968.

Françoise Van-Rossum-Guyon, *Critic of the Novel* [*Critique du roman*]. Paris: Gallimard, Collection "Bibliothèque des idées," 1971.

Lucien Dallenbach, *The Book and its Mirrors in the Work of M. B.* [*Le livre et ses miroirs dans l'œuvre de Michel Butor*]. Paris: Minard, "Archives des Lettres Modernes," 1972.

François Aubral, *Michel Butor*. Paris: Seghers, Collection "Poètes d'aujourd'hui," 1973.

André Helbo, *Michel Butor, Towards a Literature of the Sign* [*M. B., Vers une littérature du signe*]. Brussels: Editions Complexe, 1975.

Jennifer Waelti-Walters, *Michel Butor*. Victoria, Canada: Sono Nis Press, 1977.

Dossiers, special issues of journals:

L'Arc, No. 39, *Butor*, 1969.

Colloquium of Cerisy. 10/18, No. 902, conducted by Georges Raillard, 1974.

Magazine littéraire, No. 110, March 1976, *Michel Butor*, coordinated by Michel Sicard.

World Literature Today, volume 56, No. 2, 1982. *Michel Butor Issue*, organized by Ivar Ivask.

Texte en main, No. 2, 1984. *To Write with Butor* [*Ecrire avec Butor*]. Coordinated by Clairette Oriol-Boyer.

To See with Michel Butor [*Voir avec Michel Butor*]. Liège, 1984.

Kentucky Romance Quarterly, volume 32, No. 1, 1985. *Butor Studies*, coordinated by Germaine Baril.

Treatment of the Text [*Traitement de texte*]. Gourdon: Dominique Bedou, 1985.

APPENDIX

ENGLISH TRANSLATIONS

Acknowledgment: I would like to express my appreciation to Professor Bodo Richter, Emeritus, SUNY-Buffalo, for providing me with his own copy of F. C. St. Aubyn, *The William J. Jones Collections: Rimbaud—Butor* (Springfield, Missouri: Friends of the Southwest Missouri State Libraries, 1986) published in limited edition, without which this bibliography could not have been assembled.

Books:

Degrees. [*Degrés*]. Tr. Richard Howard. London: Methuen, 1962.

Description of San Marco [*Description de San Marco*]. Tr. Barbara Mason. Fredericton, Canada: York Press, 1983.

Extraordinary Tale, Essay on a Dream of Baudelaire's [*Histoire extraordinaire*]. Tr. Richard Howard. London: Jonathan Cape, 1969.

Milan Passage [*Passage de Milan*], Chapters VII-X. Tr. Guy Daniels. Gil Orlovits, ed., *The Award Avant-Garde Reader.* New York: Award Books, 1965.

Milan Passage, Chapters XI-XII. Tr. Donald Schier. *The Carleton Miscellany,* No. 3 (Summer 1963).

Mobile, Study for a Representation of the United States. [*Mobile, Etude pour une représentation des Etats-Unis*]. Tr. Richard Howard. New York: Simon & Schuster, 1963.

Niagara [*6.810.000 litres d'eau par seconde*]. Tr. Elinor S. Miller. Chicago: Henry Regnery, 1969.

Passing Time—A Change of Heart [*La modification*]. Tr. Jean Stewart. New York: Simon & Schuster, 1969.

Painting Words [*Les Mots dans la peinture*]. Tr. Joy N. Humes. *Tri-quarterly,* No. 20 (Winter 1971).

Essays, Articles, Poetry, and Excerpts:

"The Bagatelles of Thélème." Tr. Leon S. Roudiez. *The Review of Contemporary Fiction,* No. 3 (Fall 1985).

Boomerang: "Extracts from 'The Ceremony I missed' " ["La fête en mon absence"]. Tr. Michael Spencer. *The Malahat Review,* No. 60 (October 1981).

Boomerang: Letters from the Antipodes. Tr. Michael Spencer. Athens, Ohio: Ohio University Press, 1981.

"The Conversation, On Some Pictures by Alessandro Magnasco (1957)." Tr. Edward Lucie-Smith. Simon Watson Taylor, ed. *French Writing Today.* Harmondsworth: Penguin, 1968.

"Criticism and Invention" ["La critique et l'invention"]. Tr. Jean Garagnon and Graeme Watson. *Meanjim Quarterly,* No. 119 (Summer 1969).

"Delphi." Tr. Richard Howard. *Evergreen Review,* No. 18 (May-June 1961).

"Growing Pains in Science Fiction" ["La crise de croissance de la science-fiction"]. Tr. Donald Schier. *The Carleton Miscellany,* No. 3 (Summer 1963).

Inventory. 15 essays from *Repertory* I-III [*Répertoire*] and *Spirit of the Place* [*Le génie du lieu*]. New York: Simon & Schuster, 1968.

"Laundry for Marie-Jo" ["La lessive de Marie-Jo"]. Tr. Karlis Racevskis. *Antioch Review,* Vol. 45, No. 3 (Summer 1987).

"The Mosques of New York, or The Art of Mark Rothko" ["Les mosquées de New-York ou l'art de Mark Rothko"]. Tr. Richard Howard. *New World Writing,* No. 21 (1962).

"Nine Classics of Japanese Art (From Floatings from East to West)" ["Flottements de l'est en ouest"]. Tr. Terese Lyons. *SubStance,* No. 33/34, X: 4 (1981)/XI: 1 (1982).

"On Flaubert's *Bouvard and Pécuchet*" (last chapter of *Improvisations sur Flaubert* [*Improvisations on Flaubert*]). *The Review of Contemporary Fiction,* No. 3 (Fall 1985).

"The Opera, that is to say, The Theater" ["L'opéra, c'est-à-dire le théâtre"]. Tr. C. J. Beyer. *The Opera Journal,* No. 2 (Spring 1968).

"Réminiscences du corbeau/The Raven's Reminiscences." Tr. Leon S. Roudiez. *The Review of Contemporary Fiction,* No. 3 (Fall 1985). Also in *World Literature Today,* No. 2 (Spring 1982).

"Smoke Signals" ["Signaux de fumée"]. Tr. Leon S. Roudiez. *The Review of Contemporary Fiction,* No. 3 (Fall 1985).

The Spirit of Mediterranean Places [*Le génie du lieu*]. Tr. Lydia Davis. Marlboro, Vermont: Marlboro Press, 1986.

"The Sources of Contemporary Art" ["L'art contemporain jugé par ses sources"]. Tr. Jean Stewart. The London Magazine, No. 4 (July 1961).

"Zola's Blue Flame" ["Emile Zola romancier expérimental et la flamme bleue"]. Tr. Michael Saklad. *Yale French Studies,* No. 42 (1969).